How to Grow Your Business

For Entrepreneurs

PEARSON
Prentice Hall
BUSINESS

Books that make you better

Books that make you better. That make you *be* better,
do better, *feel* better. Whether you want to upgrade your
personal skills or change your job, whether you want to improve
your managerial style, become a more powerful communicator,
or be stimulated and inspired as you work.

Prentice Hall Business is leading the field with a new breed of
skills, careers and development books. Books that are a cut
above the mainstream – in topic, content and delivery – with an
edge and verve that will make you better, with less effort.

Books that are as sharp and smart as you are.

Prentice Hall Business.
We work harder – so you don't have to.

For more details on products, and to contact us, visit
www.pearsoned.co.uk

Praise for How to Grow Your Business for Entrepreneurs

'This book captures what entrepreneurs need to know to break through their own glass ceilings and to grow their businesses. Written in eminently readable style – whether you're an entrepreneur or director of a small company – you need to read this book.

There are so many great ideas in this book – make sure your first action plan is to read a section, implement it, then come back for more!'

DR SHAI VYAKARNAM, DIRECTOR, CENTRE FOR ENTREPRENEURIAL

LEARNING, JUDGE BUSINESS SCHOOL,

UNIVERSITY OF CAMBRIDGE

'If you want a practical guide to making your mark and taking your business to the next level, read this book before your competitors do.'

DR SALLY ERNST, UK PRESIDENT,

ENTREPRENEURS' ORGANISATION

'This book is a toolkit for entrepreneurs. It contains so many exercises in analysis and thinking that are applicable at the different stages of growing a business. Alex Blyth clearly recognises that entrepreneurs are short of time and offers practical steps and guidelines'.

RESHMA SOHONI, CEO, SEEDCAMP

How to Grow Your Business

For Entrepreneurs

Alex Blyth

PEARSON
Prentice Hall
BUSINESS

Harlow, England • London • New York • Boston • San Francisco • Toronto • Sydney • Singapore • Hong Kong
Tokyo • Seoul • Taipei • New Delhi • Cape Town • Madrid • Mexico City • Amsterdam • Munich • Paris • Milan

PEARSON EDUCATION LIMITED

Edinburgh Gate
Harlow CM20 2JE
Tel: +44 (0)1279 623623
Fax: +44 (0)1279 431059
Website: www.pearsoned.co.uk

First published in Great Britain in 2009

© Pearson Education Limited 2009

The right of Alex Blyth to be identified as author of this work has been asserted by him in accordance with the Copyright, Designs and Patents Act 1988.

ISBN: 978-0-273-72093-5

British Library Cataloguing-in-Publication Data
A catalogue record for this book is available from the British Library

Library of Congress Cataloging-in-Publication Data
Blyth, Alex
   How to grow your own business for entrepreneurs / Alex Blyth.
      p. cm.
   Includes index.
   ISBN 978-0-273-72093-5 (pbk.)
   1. Entrepreneurship. 2. Success in business. I. Title.
   HB615.B63 2009
   658--dc22
                                       2009017899

10 9 8 7 6 5 4 3 2 1
13 12 11 10 09

Series text design by Design Deluxe
All cartoons © Jurgen Wolff
Typeset in 9/13pt, Swis721 Lt BT by 30
Printed and bound in Great Britain by Henry Ling Ltd, Dorchester, Dorset

The publisher's policy is to use paper manufactured from sustainable forests.

Contents

...for Entrepreneurs

Being an entrepreneur can be the path to controlling your own life and to financial success. With the *For Entrepreneurs* series, it doesn't have to be a lonely journey any more. Our expert authors guide you through all phases of starting and running a business, with practical advice every step of the way. Whether you are just getting started or want to grow your business, whether you want to become a skilled marketer or salesperson or just want to get your business finances under control, there is a *For Entrepreneurs* book ready to be your experienced, friendly and supportive business coach. Our titles include:

→ *How to Start Your Own Business for Entrepreneurs*

→ *How to Grow Your Business for Entrepreneurs*

→ *Selling for Entrepreneurs*

→ *Marketing for Entrepreneurs*

→ *Book-keeping and Accounts for Entrepreneurs*

You'll find more information and more support on our website: **www.forentrepreneursbooks.com**.

Jurgen Wolff, General Editor

About the author

Alex Blyth is a freelance journalist who has spent many years writing for publications in the small business sector, such as *Director*, *First Voice*, *New Business*, *Accountancy*, *PR Week*, *Retail Week*, *Print Week* and so on. You can find out more about him, and read hundreds of his published articles, at **www.alex-blyth.co.uk**.

As well as a prolific writer, Alex is an award-winning public speaker, and is regularly called upon to speak at conferences, product launches and workshops. He also runs a series of monthly open training courses on PR skills, such as writing effective copy, getting coverage in the business press and successful media interviews.

Before he became a freelance journalist he was a director at a small business in central London. He recruited, trained and managed a team of 20 people and was responsible for a client base worth £1.5 million. During that time he tackled many of the issues that he now covers in his articles and books.

Alex lives in south west London with his wife. He spends a lot of time running around Tooting Common, and continues to support Tottenham Hotspur FC, more in hope than expectation.

Introduction

You want to increase turnover and profits, but you're too busy working for your business to even think about how to do it, much less do it. Every day you face the challenges of rising material costs, a mounting tax and regulatory burden, increased international competition, an ever more challenging labour market and customers who seem to become more and more demanding every time you speak to them.

Furthermore, there just isn't the advice out there to help you do it. If you want to set up a business you will quickly find yourself surrounded by people wanting to advise you. Go into any bookshop and you will find shelves groaning with books about how to set up a business and survive those difficult early years. Yet, once you've done that and are established on a solid footing, wanting to grow further, suddenly all the advice dries up. Sure, you can hire a consultant to advise you in this area, but chances are you don't have the thousands of pounds spare that those consultants charge.

That's where this book comes in.

This book aims to provide you with the advice you need to take your enterprise to the next level. It will show you how to find new customers, how to keep existing customers, how to cut operating costs, how to cope with all the red tape and how to get your staff working more productively.

It is not an academic textbook. It will not give you anodyne processes and glib acronyms. It will provide you with practical advice for steps you can take right now, with the minimum financial investment, to grow your business.

This isn't a workbook, and while there is a logical flow to the chapters in the book, there is nothing to stop you tackling them in any order you want. Maybe you just want to get some great ideas for how to promote your business online? Then go straight to Chapter Nine – by the end of it you'll know how to produce marketing emails that people will want to read, you'll know how to get your website higher up search engine rankings and you'll know how to produce and promote a blog.

Dip into any chapter and you'll find it bursting with that sort of practical advice, all of which is geared towards helping you grow your business.

In fact this book could change your life.

The principles and methods we'll cover have been applied with success by many entrepreneurs. One who has faced similar issues is Tom Gorman, the managing director of TDG Print, a London-based print management firm. 'Ten years ago I thought I'd taken my business as far as it could go,' he says. 'I'd set the company up a few years earlier, and had relied heavily on my sales skills to win a few good clients and achieve a respectable turnover and profit.'

It had been hard work getting his enterprise off the ground. As anyone who has ever set up a business knows, those early years are always difficult and not everyone survives them. Many new businesses fail in their early years, so entrepreneurs like Tom Gorman who succeed in establishing a new business are right to feel proud of their achievements.

But, once you've done that – what next?

The dilemma

What to do next was also what Tom Gorman wondered back in 1998. He'd achieved his initial goals of getting the business off the ground, but how could he take it on to the next stage?

He recalls: 'I knew the business concept had potential. We buy print on behalf of our clients, so they don't need to have a print buying overhead, and can get lower prices on their print through our bulk buying capabilities. It's a great business model, and was a rapidly growing market. My problem was that my company seemed to have reached a plateau.'

'I had some bright, dynamic staff, but somehow nothing seemed to get done when I wasn't there to do it. Even though we were always winning new customers, we'd reached a point where our turnover was stuck, and we just weren't growing any more. I was working every hour in the day, and plenty in the night, and my business was ruling my life. But despite this, and despite having such a great business model, we just weren't progressing. It was incredibly frustrating.'

You are not alone

Tom Gorman's situation was far from unique. You might recognise some of his experiences. They're much more common than is generally realised.

There are 1.2 million businesses in the UK with between one and 50 employees. They employ 47.5 per cent of the UK's workforce and generate 37.4 per cent of the country's income.[1] They're a crucial part of the economy. And yet, many of those companies are stuck. Some get bought by larger competitors, and a few do manage to grow, but the vast majority remain stuck in the middle ground.

Many are happy there. There are thousands of small business owners who are happy to keep things ticking over, bringing in a respectable income, and providing a good lifestyle. If that's you then this book isn't for you. Hopefully you haven't spent any of your hard-earned money on it. You can put it back on the shelf (in a prominent position, please, so passers-by can see it), and I wish you well.

However, if you are an entrepreneur, if you do want to move your business on to the next level, but, like Tom Quillan, you're struggling to make it happen, then this book *is* for you.

I know how hard it can be to make that next step. As a freelance journalist who writes for the small business and trade media, I meet and interview hundreds of entrepreneurs like you every year. Before making the move into journalism I was a director at a sales and marketing agency in central London. When I joined the company it employed around ten people, had a turnover of around £1 million and, despite having a great niche and some talented and committed staff, struggled for years to move on to the next level.

I've experienced the frustration at first hand, and since then I've seen hundreds of other entrepreneurs wrestling with exactly the same problems.

Do you want to find out what happened to the one I mentioned above, Tom Gorman? Well, we'll get there in the end. You'll find the outcome of that story at the end of the book. All I'll say for now is that it has a happy ending.

---

[1] Office of National Statistics, 2007, **http://stats.berr.gov.uk/ed/sme/smestats2007-ukspr.pdf.**

Despite all the difficulties you face, there is absolutely no reason why your business story can't have a happy ending as well – and this book is going to show you how. Follow the advice in the following pages, and before you know it you'll no longer be working for your business, it will be working for you. It will be hard work getting there. It always is. But, believe me, it'll be worth it.

Getting ready to grow

Part One

Before beginning, plan carefully.

Cicero

Turn your dreams into reality

Chapter One

It's not just for start-ups – why planning matters

You probably have a business plan. Most likely it's somewhere in your office – on your hard drive or in a drawer in a filing cabinet. You can remember those long hours you spent writing it when you set up your business. You had clear targets for your first year, and you had a strategy for how you were going to meet those targets.

But that was then, and this is now. You're not running a fledgling business any more, so you don't need to waste time on plans, right? You've got to get stuck into the hard work of finding customers, delivering to them, managing staff, controlling finances and so on.

Like many recently established entrepreneurs you probably see planning as a luxury you can no longer fit into your busy schedule. Or you think of business plans as sales tools for generating external investment, useful when setting up or selling, but not really relevant for all the years in between.

In fact, nothing could be further from the truth – you need a plan now more than ever.

When you first started out it was of course a good idea to have a plan, but chances are that much of it went out the window in your first week of trading. Before you set up your business you were only guessing at what you would sell, who you would sell it to, the channels you would use, the prices you would charge and so on.

Your plan served as a useful guide, but it soon changed when you discovered that your product sells better in France than you thought it would, or that you're having more success selling to the trade than retail, or that you've over-priced your consultancy services, and so on.

However, now that you're up and running, you are much better placed to write a plan that you really can follow. And you need to write one for exactly the same reasons as you needed to write one when your business was still on the drawing board – if you know where you want to get to, you are much, much more likely to get there.

In the words of the often-quoted but rarely considered aphorism: 'To fail to plan is to plan to fail.'

The absence of a plan for growth is one of the main factors holding back so many enterprises. It is critical that you have one. In this chapter

I am going to show you how to make one. It's not going to be any old plan either. You're not just going to scribble it down on the back of a beer mat. You're going to research it thoroughly, think about it deeply and then express it clearly. It's going to be the blueprint for growing your business.

Finding time for planning

Planning won't take a huge amount of time – probably around half a day to start with – but you do need to set aside that time to do it.

I know how hard this can be. You're a busy person, constantly under pressure to deliver to customers, keep production ticking over, manage staff, and do all of the tasks that keep your business running. You don't have half a day to spend on a luxury like planning. However, you need to make it a priority. If you don't act on it now, you'll probably never get round to doing it. You'll read a little more of this book, maybe get to the end of this chapter, then put it aside – and then you'll be caught up in the day-to-day running of your business. I've done it myself. I've seen hundreds of other entrepreneurs make this mistake. *Don't put off planning – do it now!*

" A good plan today is better than a perfect plan tomorrow. GEORGE PATTON

Right now, with this book in your hands, you have a golden opportunity to grow your business and revolutionise your life. In ten years' time, once you have transformed your business, you will look back at this moment as the one where it changed.

Open your diary and look at your schedule for the next month. Then find an hour a week for four weeks that you can dedicate to planning the future of your business.

Don't block out a whole day or a half-day for this planning. In my experience this tends to result in senior managers sitting in a conference room somewhere staring blankly at a flipchart, brows furrowed as they try to work out what their strengths, weaknesses, opportunities and threats are. These sessions rarely produce results.

It's far better to spread your planning out over four weeks. Do an hour a week, make some progress, then leave it. In between your planning sessions you'll be able to do any research you might need to do, but most importantly you'll have time to think through your thoughts.

Often our best planning isn't done in a planning session, but when we're lying in a bath, pounding a treadmill or sitting in the hairdressers. By spreading your planning out in this way you'll give yourself a chance to really think through where you are now, where you want to get to and how you're going to get there.

Once you've allocated time in your diary to planning, make sure you stick to those times. Don't be tempted to get sucked back into the day-to-day work. All those everyday tasks are important – they're what keep your business ticking over – but in the long term they are not nearly as important as the planning work you're about to do.

Getting started – setting a goal

Business planning really is a fairly simple process. It's about working out where you are now and where you want to be in the future.

The place to start is with the numbers. Ultimately that's what we're about here – growing the numbers. Take up your pen now and write down your turnover and net profit for the past three years:

Year			
Turnover			
Net profit			

Now, think about where you would like to be in the long term. Traditionally when we speak of the long term in business we're talking about ten years from now. However, it may be that you want to sell your business in five years or you want to build it up until you retire in 20 years. In this book we're working on achieving your personal goals, not on fitting you into a theoretical straitjacket.

Don't worry at this point about being realistic. Just write down your long-term objective for your company's turnover and net profit:

Year	
Turnover	
Net profit	

So, now that we know your goals, we can start developing a plan to achieve them.

" Always think ahead – it wasn't raining when Noah built the Ark. RICHARD CUSHING

To build this plan you need to get a clear picture of your business as it is now. Begin by considering your product, people and market.

1 What do you sell?

2 Who makes it (or delivers it if you sell a service)?

3 Who sells it?

4 Who buys it?

In order to grow your turnover and profit you need to change one or more of those factors. It can be internal: you can work on a strength or correct a weakness. Or it can be external: you can take advantage of an opportunity or side-step a threat that others fall into.

In order to grow it may be simply that you need to increase the quantity of people making or delivering your goods. Or you might need to make more fundamental changes, say to your sales process or your target audience, or even to the product you are selling.

To be certain about what you need to change – to come up with the right plan – you need to have a crystal clear understanding of your product and your company and how they fit into your market.

Swotting pests – two simple but effective planning techniques

I know I promised that I won't be boring you with anodyne acronyms, but at this stage I'm going to ask you to bear with me, as there are three of these techniques that I do believe are very useful for business planning. The first two are the SWOT and PEST models. The third, introduced later in this chapter, is SMART. I promise that after this planning chapter, this book will be entirely free of catchy acronyms!

SWOT analysis

A SWOT analysis is a great way of understanding your business and its potential. It stands for:

→ **S**trengths

→ **W**eaknesses

→ **O**pportunities

→ **T**hreats

So, I'd like you to spend some time now thinking about:

→ What strengths do you have that you can build on?

→ What opportunities exist that you can exploit?

→ What weaknesses can you identify and correct?

→ What threats are looming that you can avoid?

Within those four broad categories you can ask yourself more specific questions, such as:

→ If you have a product that is first to market, how can you use this strength?

→ If you struggle to recruit enough good staff, how can you correct this weakness?

→ If your services are increasingly in demand in the growing environmental markets, how can you exploit this opportunity?

→ If your manufacturing process is soon to be heavily regulated by the European Union, how can you avoid this threat?

Look at each aspect of your business – the product, people, market – and think about its current strengths and weaknesses and the threats and opportunities it may face over the next decade. Write them down.

	Product	*People*	*Market*
Strengths			
Weaknesses			
Opportunities			
Threats			

What you put in those boxes will depend entirely on your business, your market and your goals. However, the following questions might prompt some thoughts on your specific strengths, weaknesses, opportunities and threats:

→ Which staff could your business not survive without?

→ What is your process for developing new products?

→ How do you recruit new staff?

→ What percentage of your staff left in the last year?

→ What are your three largest areas of expenditure?

→ Which are your most important suppliers?

→ What percentage of your customers did you lose in the last year and why did you lose them?

→ How do you acquire new customers?

→ In the past year have you gained or lost market share against competitors?

→ What legislation is on the horizon that could affect your business?

→ Where will competition come from?

Danger!

You will only get so far on your own. You may need to convene a brainstorming session with your senior management, possibly with everyone in your company. If you do go down this route, try to stimulate as many ideas as possible. If someone suggests something, resist the immediate temptation to evaluate the idea – write it down and consider it more carefully afterwards.

You will probably find it easier to identify your strengths and weaknesses than the opportunities and threats you face. This is because we tend to be so consumed with running our business that we lack the time or focus to really consider external factors that might affect our businesses. You, like me, probably know entrepreneurs who work in the property sector and who were so busy in the booming market of the past few years that they failed to consider how the market and the broader economy could change. Many of them are now wishing they had taken the time to consider those external influences, and maybe diversify, before the bottom fell out.

A useful PEST

This is where the second acronym comes in: the PEST model will help you to identify the external changes you will face in the coming years and how they will affect your business. It stands for:

→ Politics

→ Economics

→ Society

→ Technology

What political changes might occur that could affect your business? Is a change of government at a national or local level likely? What new laws are on the horizon? Think about European as well as UK legislation in areas such as employment, taxation, industry-wide regulation and so on.

What economic changes can you predict? How would it affect your business if interest rates were to rise 100 per cent, say from 2 per cent to 4 per cent? What lies ahead for the housing market, the cost of food and energy, levels of personal taxation, and how might this affect your customers' willingness to spend their money?

Social trends can be harder to predict, but when you get it right it reaps dividends – just look at the success of Anita Roddick, who spotted the growing enthusiasm for ethically produced cosmetics and made a fortune from The Body Shop. Think about how society is likely to change in the coming years. Will it age? Where will we live? What will we do in our leisure time?

How to Grow Your Business for Entrepreneurs

Finally, we're all aware of how technology can transform a business almost overnight. In 1975 Bill Gates, Paul Allen and Ric Weiland made just over $16,000 from their fledgling enterprise, but they had spotted a technological trend, and we all know how well that one worked out. What new technologies are coming through now that could provide opportunities or threats to your enterprise?

As with the SWOT analysis, you may want to conduct a company-wide brainstorming session on the PEST factors. You will almost certainly need to spend some time researching before you have a clear picture of the political, economic, social and technological developments that will affect your business, and consequently a clear picture of your business's strengths and weaknesses and the opportunities and threats it will face in the years ahead.

Once you have done this work, it should be apparent to you what you need to do to achieve your goals. At the very least you should be able to identify one thing you can change that will enable you to grow your business.

If you've not been able to identify anything, maybe your business has already reached its optimum potential. If that is the case, congratulations – maybe you should start a new one?

Very few businesses, however, are unable to improve or develop in any way, and so it's almost certain that you have identified areas for change.

This is the point at which you should go back and look at your figures. Are they realistic? Can you really achieve that in ten years? Is the opportunity great enough? Are you really that strong? Will correcting that weakness make enough of a difference?

Perhaps you've been overly cautious in your financial goals. Either way, you need to spend time devising realistic targets for your business. Do the maths. Consider all the factors. Make them realistic but ambitious.

Now you should have:

1 Your long-term targets for turnover and profit.

2 A list of what you will change to achieve that.

Good work! You know where you are going and how you are going to get there – you have a plan.

Be careful what you wish for – it might just come true

Your plan should excite you. If it's a good plan, it should have got you fired up, champing at the bit to get out there and make it happen.

However, it probably also makes you a little scared. If you've done this planning process properly, you've probably projected yourself into your own future and seen the realisation of all your business wishes. You may have seen yourself at the point where you're no longer working for your business, but your business is working for you, where you are at last free to do what you want with your life.

They say we should be careful what we wish for, and while those of us who run small businesses usually want nothing more than to make them a success and to be free from the day-to-day fire-fighting, it is common for us to become addicted to it.

Just as the corporate executive who has worked from nine until six, commuting on the same train every day for 40 years, looking forward to retirement, struggles to cope with that retirement when it does come, so the entrepreneur, who spends years giving their all to building a business, can miss the excitement when success finally comes.

Prepare for it. While you plan the future of your business or of your career, plan for your personal future. Think about what you will do when you have implemented this long-term plan. Will you set up another business? Will you travel the world? Or will you just spend more time

How to Grow Your Business for Entrepreneurs

with your family? Whatever it is, know what you want to do and start planning for it now.

Knowing that your life will change is very different from preparing for it. You need to find time to get yourself ready, mentally and physically. But you are unlikely to have time at work for a luxury like this. Instead, build time into your daily routine to think about it. When you're in the shower, on the way into work or out on a run, try to picture yourself once you've realised your business objectives.

What will your life be like? What will you do from day to day? By building up a mental image of your new life in this way you will acclimatise yourself to it, and will be able to make any plans necessary to ensure you fully enjoy the fruits of your labour.

A SMART one-year plan

You need to translate your long-term plan into something more manageable. You need to produce a plan for year one of your new future.

Doing this is relatively straightforward – look at your long-term plan and decide what you must achieve in the next 12 months in order to be on track to meet that long-term plan – but you have to think carefully about it. At this stage you need to nail down concrete objectives that are going to guide and motivate you tomorrow, the next day and so on until you've met your long-term goals. If your short-term objectives are vague, unrealistic or too easy, they won't help you.

A goal without a plan is just a wish.

ANTOINE DE SAINT-EXUPERY

This is where I want to introduce the final acronym. When you devise your one-year objectives you need to ensure that every one is SMART:

→ **S**pecific – be clear what it relates to

→ **M**easurable – know exactly what constitutes success

→ **A**mbitious – make sure it stretches your business

→ **R**ealistic – ensure you can actually achieve it

→ **T**ime-based – give it a deadline so you have a date to work towards

Once you have a clear idea of your one-year plan, you can break it down into a plan for the next month. Again ensure your objectives are SMART.

Finally, you can plan what you will do next week and tomorrow. By taking this approach, you will know that when you wake up tomorrow morning you're making a start on your long-term plan. The plan isn't something nebulous in the future – it is a set of clear, actionable objectives for you to achieve tomorrow, in the next week, the next month, the next year.

Danger!

It's a human tendency to vastly overestimate what we can achieve in a day, and underestimate what we can achieve in a year. Don't aim to do too much in a day and then get disappointed in yourself. The best way to achieve your goals is to make small steps in the right direction day after day after day.

Danger

Revisit it – the best plans are flexible

The best-laid plans of mice and businessmen are always thrown off course. You cannot hope to have predicted all the changes to the global economy, the tax regime, competitor activity and so on that will happen in the next few years, possibly in the next few months. You will also find that what you want will change in the future.

However, this does not mean that you should never have a plan, that you should allow yourself to be buffeted by external forces and to change direction with your own moods. On the contrary, you must always have a clear direction of where you are going, and you must regularly review this plan to ensure it remains relevant.

Put aside an hour, two if you can spare them, every month to revisit your plan. See how you have performed against your monthly objectives, evaluate what went right and what went wrong, and make sure you are clear about why. Review your long-term objectives in the light of what has happened that month, and then look at your one-year plan and your plan for next month.

How to Grow Your Business for Entrepreneurs

In this way, planning will become integral to everything you do. You will always know where you are headed, and you will have a much greater chance of getting there.

It's a plan, not a secret

While your business plan is very much about you and your personal goals, remember that it will affect everyone involved in your business. Tell them about it.

When you're devising your plan, talk to any fellow shareholders about the long-term personal goals that you are aiming towards. Find out what theirs are, and talk to them about how the plan will help them achieve those goals.

Also involve your employees at every stage. They will bring a fresh perspective to your strengths, weaknesses, opportunities and threats, and will help you build an accurate picture.

Once you have written your plan, communicate it to everyone in your business. Let them know what your annual targets are, and show them how their input will contribute directly to achieving those goals.

Finally, give everyone a good reason to want to make that contribution. Show them how their career will develop, or take everyone out for an end-of-year party. Whatever you do, remember that you won't be able to achieve your goals on your own.

In the next chapter you'll see how you can get the most out of those employees through successful delegation, but first let's see how the methods described in this chapter worked for one company.

Case study
Pure

'When Microsoft started out, the team there had a very clear mission,' says Darren Fell, Sussex Entrepreneur of the Year 2007–08. 'They wanted Windows to be the operating system on every computer in the world. When I started Pure back in 2001, I tried to set out with that level of clarity. I wanted to become the standard for email marketing.'

Back then, he was operating from his spare room, he had remortgaged his flat and he had taken out every credit card, loan and overdraft he could get his hands on. He was determined that his business was going to succeed and he had a very clear plan for how it was going to happen.

He says: 'When I started out with Pure I laid down specific, time-based targets, and I knew how I was going to achieve them. I can't pretend that I met every one of those targets. All good plans are flexible, and very often in business it takes longer than you expect to achieve your goals, but having the plan in place meant I always knew where I was going.'

This meticulous planning certainly produced results for him – Pure now has more than 800 clients including the *Financial Times* and Innocent Drinks. The company was listed in 2007 as the eleventh fastest growing new media business in the UK, and in April 2008 Fell sold Pure for $7.8 million.

A serial entrepreneur, Fell began working on his next venture while he was still running Pure. In his evenings and weekends he developed the concept for Crunch, an online accounting system aimed specifically at the rapidly growing freelance and contractor market. It launched in November 2008.

He is applying the same careful planning to this new venture, aiming to reach £5.5 million turnover and £1 million profit within three years. 'Once you've got to the £1 million profit level larger companies start taking you seriously as an acquisition target. It's important to plan your growth to get to that level before you can even consider any sort of exit strategy.'

His success is by no means solely due to planning. He also advises other entrepreneurs to innovate constantly to ensure that their products and services stand out from the competition. He believes strongly in diversification to reduce reliance on one client or one sector, and he warns against allowing the 'money men' to cut costs at the expense of providing outstanding customer service.

He is, though, a vigorous advocate of business planning. He concludes:

'Very often in my experience the reason why companies plateau is they don't have clear financial goals or a plan for achieving them. Entrepreneurs who want to grow their businesses need to spend time getting plans in place, and then be prepared to revisit and recast those plans regularly.'

Key points

→ Set aside one hour every month to focus on your long-term plan.

→ Give yourself a long-term financial goal to work towards.

→ Conduct SWOT and PEST analyses to understand your current situation and your operating environment.

→ Decide on at least one thing you can change to progress towards your long-term financial goal.

→ Consider how your life will change once you have achieved your goal.

→ Produce a one-year plan with SMART objectives.

→ Revisit your plan once a month.

→ Communicate your plan to everyone it will affect.

Next steps

What action will you take to apply the information in this chapter? By when will you do it?

_____

_____

_____

_____

No person will make a great
business who wants to do it
all himself.

Andrew Carnegie

You're not alone – delegate to grow

The biggest barrier to the growth of your business

What do you think is the biggest obstacle to the growth of your business? Is it the competition? Is it the rising cost of raw materials? Is it excessive red tape?

In actual fact it is very possible – likely even – that the single, most significant obstacle to growth is the owner, the entrepreneur who got it all started in the first place. In other words, *you*.

This is where you might decide to put this book down. I wouldn't blame you. You probably don't want to be told that the business you've sweated over for years, the business that you've grown from nothing, is now being held back and it's all your fault.

However, I'd urge you to read on just a little further.

Over the years I have seen countless small businesses where this is the case. In fact I think it is a natural stage in the growth of almost every company. It happens because entrepreneurs like you are usually very talented, self-reliant people, who have the spark of an outstanding idea and then the drive to turn that idea into reality.

The problem is that they rarely have either the inclination or the ability to make the transition from pioneer to empire-builder, from entrepreneur to managing director.

It is, after all, an entirely different role. You wouldn't ask a Formula One driver to conduct an architectural survey of your house, so why should you expect someone who starts companies to be able to manage a company's growth?

One sets out alone, with nothing but a vision and the determination to make it reality. The other is prepared to grind out a strategy, getting the best out of those around them, and carefully assembling the empire, piece by steady piece. It is extremely rare to find one person who is able to do both. Pioneers tend to get bored quickly and empire-builders usually lack the spark of invention.

Is this the case in your company?

Consider these questions:

→ How often do your employees come up with new ideas for improving what you do?

→ How many times in the last month has something important been held up because you weren't there to move it forward?

→ How many staff do you have who've been doing the same job for a long time and might be looking elsewhere for a fresh challenge?

If you can genuinely say that your employees are innovating, that your processes operate efficiently without you and that your staff are all operating at their full potential, then you don't need to read this chapter. Skip ahead to Chapter Three, where we're going to look at how to develop the potential of those staff further.

If, though, you are one of the vast majority of entrepreneurs who are working every hour they have, paying attention to virtually every detail in their operations and wondering why their staff seem to do little other than collect their pay packets, don't worry – you are not alone, and this chapter will help you.

In many ways, this is the pivotal chapter in this book. If you can make the transition successfully from entrepreneur to managing director, if you can learn to delegate effectively, you will make everything else possible. Through what you learn in this chapter you will empower your staff to do the day-to-day running of your business. You will free up your time, so that you will be able to do all the things that will build your business – recruiting and retaining more excellent staff, keeping profitable customers, winning new customers, controlling costs and financing further expansion.

The great news is that others have done it before. Pretty much every entrepreneur who has gone on to build a large business has at some stage struggled with delegation, but has recognised the problem and then learnt how to do it well.

You can, too.

Letting go

It's really very simple – you cannot grow this business on your own. There are only so many hours in the day, and no matter how brilliant you are, you can only do so much.

You, like many entrepreneurs, probably already know this. But do you really believe it?

For many entrepreneurs the business is almost like a child. You conceived the idea, were there at its birth and nurtured it carefully through the first, most difficult weeks and months. Just like a child, it gave you sleepless nights, wrecked your social life and has probably put you in a perilous financial situation. After going through all that it can be very hard to let go.

However, just as you need to send your children to school, entrusting part of their upbringing to teachers and other adults, so you have to delegate the running of your business to your employees.

Well, actually, that's not true. You don't *have* to delegate anything at all. You can keep an iron grip on your enterprise, refusing to give others any responsibility, and remain the only one who makes any decisions. However, if you do take that approach you will struggle to grow your business.

I have seen many entrepreneurs adopt this approach. They know that they need staff so they hire them and pay them, but deep down they don't trust any of them to do anything as well as they could do it themselves. Very often they're right. It probably is the case that you are much, much better at dealing with customers, planning marketing campaigns and hiring new staff than all your staff and it will probably take much longer to teach someone how to do it than it would just to do it yourself.

However, if you never invest that time, if you never put that faith in your colleagues, you will remain stuck where you are. The size of your business will be limited to roughly what you, as an individual, can achieve. Your staff might help with basic tasks, but they'll never add a great deal to the business. They'll never suggest ways to improve the business. They'll never take the initiative. And worst of all, nothing will ever get done when you're not there. You will be continually confined to your office, wondering why you bother to employ all these people.

This is also a vicious circle. The more you assume your staff are incompetent and lazy, the less you trust them with any responsibility and the less interest they will show in your business. The more dynamic ones will move on to companies that offer them a challenge and development opportunities. The rest will sit there, watching the clock and resenting you.

So let's waste no more time. Let's make a plan for you to start delegating.

What to delegate – not just photocopying!

The most difficult stage is the first one – recognising that you need to delegate. And if you've got this far in the chapter, you've already done that and are well on the way to mastering the art of delegation.

The next step is deciding what to delegate. Very often delegation goes wrong because the person doing the delegation sees it as an opportunity to get someone else to do all the jobs they find mundane. If you've ever made this mistake you'll know that by and large the outcome is that after a few weeks you're doing the boring task again, but now you're also trying to recruit a new member of staff.

You're not going to fall into that trap. You're going to delegate not just tasks, but also responsibility. This is going to challenge your employees and help them develop. It is also going to allow you to delegate more and more over time, freeing you up to focus on growing your business.

Open your diary and get out a blank piece of paper. Go back through the last month, writing down everything you have done at work. You don't need to detail every invoice you've sent or every single phone call you've made. Try to group activities under headings such as.

→ Invoicing
→ Credit control
→ Making sales calls
→ Running staff meetings
→ Interviewing for new receptionist

You should end up with a fairly extensive list of activities that comprise your working life.

The first step is to work out which tasks already fall within the job description of one of your staff. Those are the tasks that you need to delegate immediately. You're paying someone good money to do a job and then you're doing it for them! Not only is this a waste of money, it's also demotivating for your staff, and it is taking you away from long-term developmental work.

Once you've identified the tasks that you should never have been doing in the first place, you can pick out others that it would be better for you to delegate. To do this, circle the following groups of tasks:

1 Those that are repeated on a fairly regular basis. There's little point you training a member of staff to do something that you'll only ever do once a year. You want to pick out those tasks that you do every day or every week.

2 Those that are easy to explain and do. Make sure the first tasks you delegate are those that your staff can do easily. This will help build everyone's confidence that the process works.

Picking the right delegates – skills, knowledge, time, enthusiasm

Once you've identified what to delegate, you need to decide who to delegate to. If you've been doing part of someone's job, then it's obvious who you should delegate those tasks and responsibilities to.

If you're going further and giving your staff new responsibilities, you need to think carefully about who should do them.

It's not only about the money

Don't assume that delegating means you have to pay your staff more. Frequently business owners imagine that their staff will only take on new responsibilities if paid more. This isn't necessarily true.

I'm not suggesting you should pile more and more responsibilities on to individual employees without giving them appropriate rewards. I am suggesting that pay increases shouldn't be the starting point. You need to identify the members of staff who are best suited to take on this extra responsibility, not those that are most keen to increase their pay packets.

Rather than adding to your wage bill, and to your employees' pay expectations, you're much better off getting staff onside with your long-term growth plan. Make them feel part of it with their added duties and show them how they will develop their skills in this expanded role, and then once they've shown they can perform in this new position, reward them with a pay rise. By then, you'll have had time to grow your business and so you'll be able to afford it.

How to find the best people

Begin by taking another blank sheet of paper and writing the names of all the members of staff who report directly to you.

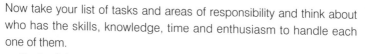

Time saver

If you've got more than six people who report directly to you, then you've already found your first area for delegation. No one can properly manage more than six people. If you're managing many more than six people then you need to hire or promote someone to manage some of them.

Now take your list of tasks and areas of responsibility and think about who has the skills, knowledge, time and enthusiasm to handle each one of them.

Each of those four criteria is vital. If any one of them is lacking, the delegation will fail. Perhaps someone is keen to get more involved in recruitment, has a good eye for detail and knows exactly what you need in new recruits. But if they're already stretched with their existing job or home commitments then they'll struggle to replace you as the person who processes incoming CVs.

You might have a talented account handler who copes with his existing workload and is keen to take over the writing of the weekly reports you send to key clients. However, if he's just joined the company and doesn't know what you include in those reports, he'll find it very difficult to do it without a great deal of hand-holding from you.

You might want to send your top salesperson, who is well ahead of her sales targets, to a conference in New York, where she can use her networking skills and knowledge of that market to make some great new contacts for your business. But if she isn't interested in doing it, you'd be better off going yourself or sending someone else.

As you can see, you need to take great care in choosing the people to whom you delegate. You may find you need to spend a few days discussing your plans with those involved, finding out whether or not they could do it or even want to do it.

You may be surprised at how much you can delegate this easily. Do you really need to compile or even approve the monthly stationery order? Does it always have to be you who opens up in the morning and locks up in the evening? Couldn't someone else manage the day-to-day contact with that client?

Training and recruiting delegates

Once you have made it work with simple tasks, move on to delegating more complex areas of responsibility. At each stage, go through the above steps to ensure you get the right person for the right task.

At some point you will find that your staff are not capable of doing more. You then need to work out what you could delegate to existing staff once they have received suitable training. Outline what that training would involve. For example, with some training, could your office manager take responsibility for invoicing and credit control? For advice on how to design and deliver a successful training and coaching programme, see Chapter Three.

Now look at what you are left with. Are there any tasks or responsibilities that you would still like to lose? How much time would it free up if you were no longer responsible for the day-to-day interaction with your customers? Are there major areas, such as managing some of the staff, where you need to bring in new people?

If this is the case, outline a job description for these new roles, and begin recruiting people to take on those areas of responsibility. To find out more about recruitment and selection tactics that will help grow your business, take a look at Chapter Four.

You might feel uneasy about this. We all like to feel as though we are indispensable, as though the business would fall apart tomorrow if we were unable to turn up. However, it's only the poorly run businesses that are that dependent on one person. Once you have mastered the art of delegation, your business will be able to function perfectly well without you. Just think what that will allow you to do. You will be able to take a holiday. You will be able to devote your energies to growing your business, rather than just keeping it ticking over day to day.

Putting it into action – communicate!

Throughout this process you must remember to keep everyone fully informed. It's not only you who will feel threatened by this process. We can all find change frightening, and unless you keep everyone up to date, your employees will start to get worried about what you're up to.

Hold a meeting. Tell everyone that this is the beginning of an exciting new phase in the company's development. Acknowledge that in the past you could have delegated more effectively, and make it clear that that is about to change. This ought to be an easy meeting. You're telling everyone that you're finally going to let them get on with their jobs, that you're not going to be interfering any more, and that this is going to have profound implications, not only for the growth of the business, but also for their individual growth.

Convey all of this and you will ensure the process begins with everyone involved and keen to see it work.

The managing director

So, that's done. You're now dispensable. Time to take that cruise round the Med, right?

Sadly not. You are still the most important person in your business. You've got a new job now – you're no longer the entrepreneur who started the business, you're the managing director who is going to lead the business's growth.

This is going to involve you in training and recruiting staff, cementing and building your customer base and bringing in finance to grow even further. Basically, it's all the exciting stuff we're going to cover in the rest of this book. But before you race ahead to the fun 'director' part of your job, you need to ensure you've nailed down the 'managing' part.

Your employees are now relying on you to manage them effectively. You might have got the right people doing the right jobs, you might have given them all the training they need, but if you fail to manage them properly you will soon find yourself back in the day-to-day maelstrom, surrounded by disillusioned staff and disgruntled customers.

The first step towards successful management is to recognise that when you delegate responsibility, you must also delegate authority.

Picture this very common scene: the entrepreneur agrees with the office manager that the office manager is now in charge of the monthly stationery order. The office manager then goes away, conducts an inventory of existing stationery and compiles an order based on previous orders and expected future need. He does, in short, exactly what he should do.

However, before he is able to email the order to the supplier, the entrepreneur pulls him aside and asks to check the order. Due to the entrepreneur's superior knowledge of how to compile the stationery order, he spots several mistakes that the office manager has made.

He tells the office manager in no uncertain terms that he needs to stop making these errors. The office manager feels as though he has failed, and the entrepreneur starts to wonder whether the office manager is really up to the job. He probably even begins to doubt the whole delegation project.

This is a depressingly common experience for many employees and employers. You've probably been there yourself as either the manager or the employee.

It's easy to see why these situations happen – no entrepreneur can afford mistakes. It's hard enough making a profit without all these staff wasting money on A5 paper that'll never be used. And that's just the tip of the iceberg, right? Imagine what else is going wrong elsewhere!

Relax. They've made a mistake, but it's probably not as bad as you think. Whenever you see one of your employees making a mistake, take a minute to consider these three points:

→ Your staff are *not* lazy. If you've got them on board with the delegation project from the outset, they will be as keen as you are to see it work. The overwhelming majority of people want to do a good job.

→ Your staff are *not* incompetent. If you've selected the right staff and have trained them properly, then they know what they're doing.

→ When you were starting your business you made mistakes. You had to figure out how to do everything. You probably over-ordered on paper at some point. Your business didn't go under as a result.

How to Grow Your Business for Entrepreneurs

The fact is that people make mistakes, particularly when they're learning. The point is to learn from those mistakes and not make them again. There are two steps you can take to help them do that.

1 Provide clear objectives

When you transfer ownership of a task or a responsibility, make it crystal clear what outcome you expect. Just as the overall business objectives you set out in Chapter One are specific, measurable, achievable, realistic and time-based, so should be those you set your staff. Try not to prescribe how they will achieve the objective. Give them the skills and knowledge to do it, and tell them how you have done it in the past, but give them the responsibility and authority for deciding how to achieve the objective.

2 Give effective feedback

Agree at the outset when you are going to review progress. Initially you will want to do this frequently, but over time you will be able to do it less and less. Stick to the meeting time, even if you are dreading what promises to be a difficult meeting. There is nothing worse for an employee who is already nervous about taking on new responsibilities than not receiving any feedback on how well it's going.

Even if you are dissatisfied with how the employee has done, you can still make it a constructive meeting with a positive outcome. Be very specific in your feedback. Explain what went well and what needs improvement, talking about behaviour, rather than personality. Avoid statements such as 'You're just doing the job badly' or 'You're too quiet to do this well'. Instead you might say: 'In the meeting with that client I felt you could have made these points more clearly.'

Once you have explained your concerns, discuss with the employee why things aren't going well. What is lacking? Does the employee need more training? Is the employee properly motivated to do the job? Do they have enough time? If you are sure that the employee has the skills, knowledge, motivation and time, but is still failing to achieve the objectives you have agreed, you might have to accept that you picked the wrong person for this role.

Danger!

Just because an individual has turned out not to be up to the job, you should not give up on delegation. It simply means you need to find someone else who is able to do this role.

Finally, remember to give positive feedback. At the performance review meeting explain what the employee is doing well. Maybe suggest areas for further improvement and development, but above all else make sure they know how much you appreciate the work they are doing for you.

Get it right and they'll want to work even harder for you. You'll have formed the core of a committed, dynamic team that is going to help you achieve the plan you made in Chapter One. You'll be ready to start growing this business. In the next chapter we'll explore how you can help your people develop their skills. First, let's look at a company that thrived when its managing director learned how to delegate effectively.

Case study
Mabox

'I've always struggled with delegation,' admits Tim Hallac, MD of Mabox, an email marketing business. 'I think I'm like many business owners out there – I'm good at what I do, but I'm not so good at managing other people.'

How to Grow Your Business for Entrepreneurs

Hallac set up Mabox in 2001 and the company grew fairly rapidly on the back of big client wins with companies like Sanyo, Reed Recruitment and UBS. By 2004 Hallac was employing 15 staff and a raft of freelancers. His annual turnover was around £700,000 and he was making around £500,000 gross profit every year.

He should have been happy at that point, having established his business, and preparing for the next stage of growth. But he wasn't. He explains: 'I had all these staff, but I just didn't trust them to do things properly. I hired account handlers, but I ended up doing all that work myself. I was working from eight in the morning until ten at night. I was constantly stressed, and I had no life. It was ridiculous – people used to come to me when the toilet roll ran out!'

He continues: 'Also, the business had stopped growing. I didn't have time to go out and win new clients, so we were stuck in a position where we were dependent on two large clients. We couldn't afford to lose them, so I ended up doing more and more of the account handling, and the situation got worse and worse.'

Fortunately, Hallac is a member of a group of business owners who meet regularly to share ideas and compare notes. He discovered that many in that group had at one time or other been in the same situation as him. So he took their advice and began to learn how to delegate.

He says: 'The first thing I did was hire two experienced account directors who I knew I could trust. Then I gave them clear key performance indicators. I made sure they were indicators that they could directly influence. Then I sat down with all my staff in one-to-one meetings and thrashed out any difficulties we had.'

He reports that there was one account handler who he always felt did things the wrong way, but that after one of these sessions in which they had a frank exchange of views Hallac realised that it was just a different way of approaching the task – it wasn't better or worse than his, just different. Since then they have worked very well together.

Putting in this work has allowed Hallac to step back from the day-to-day account handling and focus on growing the business. Turnover has grown to £1.3 million and gross profit to £900,000. Crucially, the company is no longer dependent on two clients, but has around ten regular sources of income. Hallac reports that he is now able to go on holiday for ten days, something that would have been unthinkable four years ago.

He concludes:

'Delegation allows you to have all the benefits of running a business without the downsides. It's all about recognising that your way of doing things is not the only way, and while you might be the best person to do a particular job, there are only so many hours in the day, so you have to entrust some jobs to other people.'

Key points

→ Look around your organisation and pinpoint instances where better delegation would help you grow.

→ Give yourself time to reflect on the need to let go.

→ Identify the right tasks and responsibilities to delegate.

→ Pick the right delegates.

→ Train and recruit to fill any gaps.

→ Tell everyone about this fresh start.

→ Give all staff clear objectives and performance indicators.

→ Spend time every day reviewing how well you provided feedback to your employees.

Next steps

What action will you take to apply the information in this chapter? By when will you do it?

_____

_____

_____

_____

Growing your people

Part Two

Training is everything.
The peach was once a bitter
almond; cauliflower is nothing
but cabbage with a college
education. Mark Twain

Developing skills and knowledge

Chapter Three

Mind the skills gap

It is widely recognised that the UK as a whole loses out to foreign competition because of a skills shortage. To give just a few statistics, 29 per cent of the workforce in England are not qualified to NVQ Level 2, which is the equivalent of five good GCSEs. Almost two and half million people in the workforce in England do not have any qualifications. The National Audit Office has estimated that the skills gap costs £10 billion in lost revenue each year.

How much does a lack of training cost your business? Can you honestly say that all your staff have all the skills and knowledge they need to do their jobs?

Without the necessary skills and knowledge, your staff will be unable to produce quality goods, provide good customer service or do any of the things that will make your businesses run successfully. As you grow and delegate more and more responsibility to those individuals, you need to give them more and more training.

In short, putting in place an effective training programme will be essential to growing your business, increasing your profits and revolutionising your life.

For many organisations the solution is to bring in external training consultants or to send staff on open courses. For many areas you may need to do that. However, you will be able to deliver much of the training yourself. Maybe you already do.

This chapter will give you advice on how to make that training as effective as possible. It will show you how you can, for the minimum cost, ensure that all your staff have all the skills and knowledge they need to help your business grow.

A simple, four-stage training needs analysis

You might be convinced you know what training your team needs. You might be tempted to skip this section and go straight on to the bit about how to actually deliver the training. However, take a few minutes to read this section – you might well find that your business could benefit from conducting a proper training needs analysis.

A training needs analysis allows you to align the training you provide with your business plan. It ensures that all the training is geared towards growing your business. Your gut feel might be right – it probably is in fact – but it's always worth checking.

Here are the steps to take.

Work out what jobs need to be done

You've already devised your business plan and worked out what you can delegate to whom. This should allow you to write down the responsibilities associated with every job in your organisation.

Work out what skills and knowledge are necessary to do each job

For each job in your organisation write down the skills and knowledge needed to do it. Try to separate the job from the current holder. Imagine the job being done as well as it possibly could, contributing to the growth of your company exactly as it ought to. Does it require sales skills? Do they need to understand how to use a particular piece of software?

Consider the people in those jobs

Put ticks next to the skills and knowledge that they possess. Again you may need to discuss this with them. You might find that someone actually knows much more about designing direct marketing campaigns than you thought they did, or that someone is considerably less confident at dealing with suppliers than they need to be. You may even need to design tests to discover whether or not someone has the required capabilities.

Highlight the gaps

Go through your list and circle the skills and knowledge gaps. These are the areas where you need to provide training. That's it – you have completed your training needs analysis! Was the result what you expected?

Devise training that works

Once you know what training your individual employees need, you can meet with them and agree personal development plans.

Danger!

Be careful not to impose training on your staff. Show them how it will help them do their jobs more successfully and how it will develop their careers. If your employees don't want to learn they won't, so above all else get their agreement that this training is necessary for them and will be good for them.

Then you can devise a schedule of training. You might find that some training needs to be done in groups of people with the same need, but much will be one to one.

Time saver

Delivering training is time consuming, so don't try to do too much at once. Make a plan so that you are doing something once a week, maybe for half a day. Keep that time sacred. It is crucial for the development of your team and the growth of your company. Don't let day-to-day operational priorities eat into this time. Stick to your plan.

Next, you need to write your training sessions.

Not so long ago, training was delivered in classrooms with trainers delivering day-long monologues to bored delegates. In recent years we have seen companies strive to make their training more interesting and participative, and so it has been common to see businesspeople building rafts in the Scottish Highlands or bemused delegates writing songs about their company vision.

In the same way, many companies have rushed to adopt new technologies such as interactive whiteboards, e-learning, online discussion groups, podcasts, even factsheets delivered via mobile phones.

While all this innovation is in many ways a step forward from the dull lectures of yesteryear, it can be very expensive, and not all of it makes the training any more effective. If you find this kit useful and you can afford it then by all means incorporate it into your training.

In my experience, it makes little difference whether you use classroom or on-the-job training, or whether you use the latest technology or not. What makes the difference between training that works and training that doesn't is following three golden rules – namely:

1 Focus on outcomes.
2 Tailor training to individual needs.
3 Always follow up.

We'll look at these in detail.

Focus on outcomes

Be clear about what you want to achieve with your training and ensure the people receiving it share those desired outcomes. Define the specific improvement that you want to see and you will find that everything will flow from that.

Tailor training to individual needs

Most obviously this concerns content – ensure you know the precise needs of the delegates and then cover exactly that. However, it also concerns the way you impart your knowledge. People learn in different ways. Some people learn best through activities, others like to go away and consider information, while many like practical tips and concrete action plans. Work out what works best for each individual and design your training so it works best for them.

Always follow up

The greatest single mistake companies make in training is thinking it ends at the training room door. The initial training session is only the first stage, and it must always be reinforced by on-the-job coaching. This is especially important with skills training, because skills need to be developed over time.

Talk, walk, stalk

There are many different models of skills training that you can follow. However, 'talk, walk, stalk' is a simple method that I have always found to produce rapid, measurable improvements.

The first stage in your training is to talk your staff through the skill in question. So, you describe what they need to do, explaining why it is important, outlining the stages involved and then going into detail about how to do each of those stages.

Your second stage is to walk them through it. You might demonstrate how to do it and then let them have a go. If possible break it down into small steps, so that the delegate gradually gains in confidence. You keep practising the skill together until they can do it.

Danger!

During the walk stage you need to do more than wait for the delegate to get it right. Without pointers on where they're going wrong, they'll just keep making the same mistakes, losing confidence and probably starting to make new mistakes. Instead, actively engage with them to identify where they're going wrong and provide advice on how to correct it.

Danger

The final stage is to stalk your employees as they put their new skills into practice. Plan to be present when they're using the skill, and be ready to intervene if they're getting something wrong or are about to fall flat on their faces. Make sure they know you're doing this – you don't want them to think you're spying on them, trying to catch them out.

Gradually over time you can stalk from a greater and greater distance, until you and the trainees are both entirely confident that they've grasped the skill. Your job is done – you can start to train them on a new skill.

How to Grow Your Business for Entrepreneurs

The talk, walk, stalk model is deceptively simple. Consciously apply it whenever you teach a member of staff a new skill and you'll find it will help you produce training that is well-structured, interactive and properly embedded.

If it helps, think back, for example, to when you were taught to ride a bike. I remember my dad explaining to me how it worked – that I sat there, pedalled, steered and tried to balance myself. He showed me how he did it on his bike. Then I got on to mine and promptly fell over! He picked me up, told me I'd lost my balance and suggested I look at the car at the end of the road, rather than down at the ground. I climbed back on, set off, got a few yards and steered straight into a bush. He showed me how to keep the handlebars straight, and we carried on like that, until I could cycle on my own. We went out for hours, with me cheerfully cycling, aware that my dad wasn't far away if I fell off. I did fall off many times, but eventually I was ready to try without my stabilisers and in time I was able to cycle on my own without my dad anywhere near.

If you think about it, any skill you've learnt in life has more or less followed that model, and it can work for any skill you want to impart to your staff.

Two Government-backed schemes you should know about

The UK Government is well aware of the skills shortage in the UK. It is keen to increase our productivity to that of our competitors such as the USA, France and Germany, and so it is currently investing significant sums of money in helping companies like yours to train staff. There are two schemes in particular that you should explore to see if you can benefit.

Train to Gain

This programme was launched by the Learning and Skills Council (LSC) in 2006 to help businesses ensure staff have the right skills to do the best job. A Train to Gain broker will visit your business and carry out a free training needs analysis.

The broker will match your training needs with suitable training providers and source any available funding. Furthermore, if you have fewer than 50 full-time employees you may be eligible for a contribution to your wage costs for staff while they are training.

Book a time for a Train to Gain adviser to visit your business and provide a free audit on what skills you need and what training is available to fill those needs. Either call 08000 155545 or look at **www.traintogain.gov.uk**.

Apprenticeships

There are already 400,000 apprentices in businesses across the UK, and the Government has committed more than £1 billion to increase the number of apprentice places by 2010/11.

It can be a very cost-effective way of bringing an extra pair of hands on board in the short term, and in the long term of developing a skilled expert who knows your business inside out.

Find out more about taking on an apprentice either by visiting the website of the Learning and Skills Council – **www.apprenticeships.org.uk/ wanttoemployanapprentice** – or by telephoning for a free information pack on 08000 150600.

In the next chapter you will discover some of the top ways to make certain you are hiring the right people. First, we'll take a look at a company that has benefited greatly from training its employees.

Case study
Europlus Direct

'When I launched my company back in 2004, training wasn't top of my agenda,' says Jim Hart, the founder and MD of Europlus Direct. 'I think that's the case with most new businesses. None of us had the time, or the inclination, to take charge of training.'

Initially it wasn't a problem. The company works in a very specific niche, helping IT hardware manufacturers stay on top of their customer service contracts. Its first client was IBM France, and it expanded rapidly to pick up IBM contracts in Spain, Germany and Italy.

Europlus Direct has also extended its services to other IT manufacturers through the launch of a sister company, Occident International. The two companies now employ over 30 different staff, and in 2008 had a combined turnover of around £4 million. It has ambitious growth plans and is in the process of setting up subsidiary offices in the USA and Australia.

However, as the company has grown, Hart has become increasingly aware of the need to provide staff training. He says: 'We've suffered with staff leaving the company because we didn't offer structured support. I realised that if I wanted to keep good staff I need to look after them, and a key component in that is offering training opportunities.'

He continues: 'Furthermore, the core of our business is sales, and good salespeople need training, not only to ensure they have the skills and knowledge required to hit targets, but also to keep them fully motivated.'

At the beginning of 2008 Hart employed a training and recruitment manager. Sharon Craggs has introduced a two-week intensive training programme for all new sales staff, quarterly training from IBM for all staff, ongoing team leader training and a structured training needs analysis for all staff.

This has had an immediate effect. Hart says: 'Although it is difficult to isolate the effect that increasing training has had on the business as other new things have been implemented at the same time, sales are up by 20 per cent in the six weeks since Sharon came on board.'

This has given Hart and his management team confidence that training is more than just a cost to be endured. They will be investing further in training to offer team-building days, complex sales training and NVQs. They are in the process of devising a fully structured training schedule for the entire company through to the end of 2009.

Hart offers this advice to anyone who is leading a growing business:

'Invest in training as soon as possible before staff start leaving, or before you suffer some other adverse effect. If you use any external courses, always go by recommendations. Finally, don't forget about training yourself. You might be the boss but you've still got a lot to learn, so go on courses, read books, get yourself a mentor. However you do it, never stop learning and growing.'

Key points

→ Conduct a training needs analysis.

→ Look into what free or subsidised assistance you are entitled to.

→ Devise your training sessions.

→ Deliver your training using the talk, walk, stalk principle.

Next steps

What action will you take to apply the information in this chapter? By
when will you do it?

_____

_____

_____

_____

When you hire people who are smarter than you are, you prove you are smarter than they are.

Anonymous

Hiring the best

Chapter Four

Why you need the very best employees

Most businesses stand or fall on the quality of their staff, and this is particularly true of small, growing businesses. As you grow, you need to ensure you have a reliable system for hiring the right people for your organisation, and right now you may well have found that your process of delegation has created new job vacancies in your company.

However, effective recruitment is far from easy. The best staff have their pick of the best jobs and you need to work hard to find them and then persuade them to join your organisation. You've got a lot to offer, but you still need to convince them of that. Finally, you need an effective selection process to ensure you don't make any bad hires.

For an average company the cost of recruiting the wrong person to a job is around 50 per cent of the annual salary for that position. For a growing business like yours the cost is even higher, as mistakes in this area can set your plan back by months or even years.

Many entrepreneurs are so concerned about recruitment that they throw money at the problem, bringing in headhunters, interview gurus, personality testing experts and so on. They waste vast sums on advertising that fails to produce results, and very often they end up hiring just the best available person, rather than the right person.

This chapter is going to show you how to avoid that.

Write a job specification

The first step must always be to draw up a clear job specification. It should detail what the person in this role will bring to the company, what specific responsibilities and tasks will be associated with the role and what qualities will be required to fill it successfully.

When deciding what sort of person you need you will begin by describing qualifications and experience. However, do not fall into the trap of ending there. Certainly a candidate's knowledge and past are important, but they are not as important as their attitude and future. No previous job will be identical to this one, and consequently good performance in a previous job is no guarantee of success in this one.

Very often we hire on experience and fire on attitude. We select someone who ticks all the boxes in terms of qualifications and experience, but soon discover that they're not well suited to the role. Perhaps they were used to working more independently than you want them to. Perhaps they flourished in a company where procedures were more clearly defined than they are in yours. There are any number of cultural and attitudinal issues that can affect whether or not someone will succeed in a role, so take some time to write down the personality traits and attitudes you believe will be essential to success in this role.

Time saver

Ask your existing staff to write descriptions of their current jobs. Not only will it provide you with a good start on job descriptions when hiring for similar positions, but it will also give you useful information on how they see their roles.

An offer they can't refuse

Once you are crystal clear about what you will gain from your new hire, and what you are looking for, you should spend some time outlining what your new hire will gain from you. At the most obvious level this is the salary and other benefits. However, top performers can get those at any company.

Think also about the less tangible benefits you can offer. Are your premises in a desirable part of town? Can you offer a pleasant working environment? How is your company viewed in the industry or local area? For advice on how to use your trade or local media to build a strong employer brand, see the public relations advice in Chapter Eight.

Think laterally about this. You probably have selling points you haven't even thought of. Ask your existing employees why they chose to work at your company. What long-term opportunities are there for staff? In Chapter Three we covered training, so can you offer career and personal development? In Chapter Five we will look at how to build a flexible package of benefits that motivates staff. Remember that you can also use these to motivate prospective staff to join your company.

You may find that this list comes easily to you. If that's the case, you've got an important head start in recruitment – just make sure you convey all these benefits in your recruitment.

The recruitment and selection process we'll cover in the rest of this chapter can only go so far. If your company is a genuinely unappealing prospect to the people you want to hire, you will still struggle. Take a look at the working environment, your reputation as an employer, the opportunities you're offering, your salary and benefits package and so on. Take steps now to improve them, no matter what they cost. Most businesses are only as good as the people who work in them.

Recruiting for free

You know the sort of person you want to hire and you've got a compelling offer in place. How do you find those people?

The best place to begin looking for new staff is always among your existing staff. Before you start spending any money on ads or any time sifting through CVs, look at your current team and ask yourself whether any of them could do this job. Not only will it save you time and money, but you already know they are a good fit with your organisation.

Danger!

Failing to consider internal candidates is usually a good way to generate resentment towards the new hire, something you should be keen to avoid.

The next best place to look is the grapevine. Ask everyone you know – clients, suppliers, former colleagues, friends, people you meet at industry events and so on – whether they know someone who might fit the bill. You could even consider offering a small incentive to your staff for a successful introduction. The chances are that their friends and family will be similar to them, so they could be ideal hires.

Consider where else you could network to get word out that you're hiring. Are there local organisations or clubs that could provide fertile hunting grounds? Could you use online social networks? Many recruiters now use networks such as LinkedIn, which has millions of members worldwide. It's relatively easy to build a network of your contacts' contacts, and before you know it you've got hundreds of businesspeople you can ask..

There are also free websites you can use. For example, many visitors to the UK from abroad use Gumtree (**www.gumtree.com**), and posting a job ad there can reap rewards. You will have to wade through many CVs, but it's free to try and you might find exactly the person you're looking for.

Building links with local schools and universities can ensure a steady stream of job applicants. Get in touch with them and offer to go and speak at a careers event. Offer to take on one or two students for work experience at a time when you're less busy, and you may unearth a star performer. Try to attend graduate recruitment fairs as well.

Finally, don't forget to advertise the position on your own website. You should have a regularly updated vacancies section and you should invite speculative CVs. You may not get a huge number of visitors to your site at the moment, but later in this book we'll be looking at how to change that, and you may find your jobs page becomes more valuable than you imagined.

Four steps to becoming a headhunter

Headhunting is a well-known and highly effective method for recruiting senior staff. However, the problem with headhunters is that they are expensive. It is not uncommon to pay 30 per cent of the employee's first year's salary to the headhunter, and few small businesses can afford a £15,000 fee to recruit an employee who will earn £50,000. By following the four steps below, you may find that you can fill that all-important vacancy yourself and save a lot of money.

Draw up a shortlist

Start by compiling a list of the people you know who might fit your brief. Although one of the richest sources of candidates will be your competitors, they are by no means the only ones. It pays to think laterally about where you find your candidates.

By focusing on the skills required to do the job, rather than purely on the experience traditionally associated with it, you should be able to expand the field quite considerably. Think of people you've met at industry events, or those you've read about or heard speak. If you've not met anyone, read about anyone or heard anyone speak, then it might be time to get out and start networking for these leads – see Chapter Eight for advice on how to do that.

You can also use the contacts you do have. If they've not been able to persuade any of their contacts to apply for your position, give them an easier question: ask them who they think would be really good for this job. Finally, try using the internet. Join online industry forums and see who is active and impressive there.

Do your research

For many, the secret of successful headhunting is research. When good headhunters call potential candidates they already know a lot about them. So, before you pick up the phone to the people on your shortlist, dig around a little.

Find out about their current role, how long they have been in it, the highlights of their time in it, what they were doing before, what colleagues, clients and other business contacts think of them and so on.

When you make your approach you want to be able to flatter them with the effort you've gone to, and you also want to be able to develop a conversation with them. You will only achieve these goals with proper preparation.

Pick up the phone

Once you've done this, the next step is simply to call them up. Call outside of work hours, ideally on a mobile phone, and introduce yourself immediately, telling them honestly why you're calling.

You might find that some will refuse to talk to you. Some might even go straight to their employers. Don't worry too much about that. You're not doing anything wrong. The worst that can happen is that you get on the wrong side of a competitor. So what? This is business. You're not here to make friends with your competitors. Just as customers are free to shop where they like, so employees are free to work where they like – you wouldn't worry about approaching a competitor's customers, so why worry about approaching their staff?

How to Grow Your Business for Entrepreneurs

In fact, you'll find that very few people will tell their employers about it. Most people will feel complimented and will be very happy to talk to you.

Softly, softly

Headhunters have a reputation for being aggressive. Indeed, many of them subscribe to the 'second-hand car salesman' school of thought and try at all costs to push people into unsuitable roles. It is easy to see why. Senior executives get dozens of calls every week from headhunters, most of which they dismiss. Those headhunters have to work hard to get a foot in the door and stand a chance of making their 30 per cent.

You, on the other hand, are only interested in finding the right person for the job. You will adopt the tactics of the more sophisticated headhunter and make unobtrusive, friendly calls to people. Rather than going straight in to discuss the job on the table, you will talk about how the executive is developing their career, where they see it going, what they want from their work and so on.

Most people prefer talking about themselves to listening to a salesperson talk up a job, so you will achieve a much better response this way. You may find that it takes longer and some conversations go nowhere. However, a relaxed chat over a coffee that leads nowhere now might in three years' time produce your best ever hire. Successful recruitment is a long-term game, so raise your sights beyond your immediate goal.

Recruitment advertising that works

It may well be the case that you're unable to fill your vacancies with any of these techniques. In that case you will probably need to look at recruitment advertising. There are four factors to get right with recruitment advertising:

1 Choosing the right media.
2 Getting the right deal.
3 Designing an effective ad.
4 Writing sparkling copy.

We'll now look at these in some more detail.

Choose the right media

Go into any newsagent, open any internet browser, and you'll see just how many media options you have. The quality and quantity of response your ad generates will vary greatly between different publications and websites. The simple question for you to answer is: where will the right candidates be? Find out what publications they read, which websites they visit, and that is where you should advertise.

Get the right deal

You need to invest time in this research, because choosing the wrong media can be very expensive. Online ads cost around £200–£300 and print ads can be thousands of pounds, although you should generally aim to get at least 20 per cent off the initial price you are quoted. You can usually get much better rates for repeat ads or long-term deals.

Danger!

In your negotiations make sure you know what you are paying for in terms of page positioning, ad design and copywriting.

Design an effective ad

Your ad needs to capture attention and to describe exactly what you are looking for and what you are offering. You almost certainly want to bring in a professional designer to do this for you, as paying thousands of pounds to place a poor ad is just a waste of money. You can hire a freelancer or small agency for a relatively modest investment. See Chapter Eleven on how to select the right agency and get maximum value from it.

Write sparkling copy

In the same way, what you say in your ad needs careful consideration. You might want to consider hiring a professional copywriter, but if you are confident that you can do it yourself, follow these golden rules:

→ Make *no* errors: spelling, grammar and factual errors make you look amateurish; inaccurate contact details are a disaster.

→ Provide essential information: state job title, duties and responsibilities, qualifications and experience required, personal traits, location and how to respond.

→ Avoid wordiness: many ads lose their core message amidst meaningless clichés; make every word count.

→ Sell the role: emphasise what about your job will most appeal to the right candidate.

Selecting the right people

Of course, attracting candidates is only half the recruitment and selection process – you then need to select the right candidate. However, if you have done the work earlier to develop a clear description of the qualifications, experience, skills, knowledge, personality and attitude you're looking for, then selection ought to be relatively straightforward.

You begin by eliminating those candidates that fail to meet your factual criteria – qualifications and experience – and you then interview the remainder.

Danger!

Always contact everyone who applied to let them know the outcome. Today's failed applicant could very easily be tomorrow's major customer, so be unfailingly polite and respectful to everyone who applies.

Time saver

If you are spending too much time sifting through inappropriate CVs', consider introducing an application form. You can use this as a self-selection tool by including questions on specific experience or education.

The interview is the primary selection technique for almost every company. However, it is important to recognise its limitations. It is easy for interviewers to take an immediate like or dislike to a candidate, based on their mood, the physical appearance of the candidate or some other irrelevant factor, and then to look for evidence to support this view. More often than not this happens subconsciously.

One way to avoid this is to use psychometric tests, which provide information about predicted behaviour in different circumstances. These can be carried out in person as a series of face-to-face discussions, or online with feedback provided within a couple of hours. The findings can be used to indicate a person's aptitude for certain activities and how they would react in a working environment.

Such testing is best used in conjunction with interviews. You can minimise the subjectivity of your interviews by preparing fully for them and standardising across all candidates. Work out beforehand what you will ask candidates; ensure the questions relate directly to the skills and qualities required in the role, ask them all the same questions and consider using a scoring system for all.

You should also aim to get your interviewees talking as much as possible. Ask open questions that will encourage them to tell you all about their relevant experience, their motivation for taking the job and their goals for the future. A successful interview is one in which you will be talking very little.

These two steps – using standard questions and encouraging interviewees to talk – will help to make your interviews more objective. However, bear in mind that you will probably need to work with this person very closely, and so at the end of the day you have to get on with them. Don't entirely discount your personal feelings.

Finally, remember that the interview is also an opportunity to sell your business and the job. Be clear beforehand about what will appeal to the right candidate about your job, and ensure you convey this clearly during the interview.

In the next chapter you'll find out how to inspire commitment in your staff. First, let's look at a case study that illustrates the power of effective recruiting.

Case study

The Clean Space

There are few industries where it is harder to recruit than in cleaning. Yet, by taking a revolutionary approach to his business Charlie Mowat has, in five years, built The Clean Space Partnership from just him on a laptop in the day and in rubber gloves at night, to a business servicing 450 customers in two cities and turning over £1.8 million a year.

In 2003 Mowat left a successful consulting career to set up his own business, convinced that there had to be a better way to run a cleaning company. He explains: 'The industry is notorious for treating staff badly. My philosophy is simple – if you treat staff well they'll be happy, and if they're happy your customers will be happy.'

He set up his ethical cleaning company, winning contracts at offices, gyms, spas and other commercial premises, and giving the cleaners the opportunity to part-own the contracts on which they work. Mowat believes that giving the cleaning contractor that financial and emotional stake in the job ensures that they are highly motivated to deliver.

It became clear early on that the model would work. The challenge Mowat faced was recruiting enough high-quality cleaners to meet the demand. Initially he relied on word-of-mouth recommendation. 'A positive employer brand is critical in this industry,' he says. 'If you treat just one person badly it'll get round and no one will want to come and work for you. If you treat your staff well, they'll tell their friends, and pretty soon they'll be sending in their CVs.'

In early 2008 the demand for cleaning services was so great that he had to begin advertising for staff. This brought him a flood of CVs, and he had to devise a process for picking out the good ones. If impressed with a CV, he conducts a phone interview. The next stage is for the company to present what it has to offer contractors and how it works. This is followed by one-to-one interviews and then job offers to the successful applicants.

So far the process has been successful. He has recruited 150 contractors in London and Manchester and is about to expand into Bristol. Looking ahead, he is convinced that he can transform the cleaning industry. 'There are a lot of small, very badly run companies in this sector,' he says. 'It's like estate agency was before Foxtons came in, or minicabs before Addison Lee. It really is an industry ready for change.'

Mowat offers this advice on successful recruitment: 'It's very important to begin with a clear understanding of the type of person you want to hire. Know exactly what job you're offering – the key objectives, the tasks, the remuneration – and think carefully about the sort of people who will succeed in it. Getting that straight at the outset can prevent a great many mistakes.'

He concludes:

'More than anything else, if you want to hire the best people, you need to give them a compelling reason to come and work for you. Average people just need a wage packet, but the top performers want more than that. You need to decide which type of person you want to hire.'

Web bonus

At our website, **www.forentrepreneursbooks.com**, click on the 'How to Grow Your Business' button. On the link for Chapter Four you'll find a leading headhunter talking about how he finds the right candidates and sells the job to them.

Key points

→ Decide which positions you need to recruit for.

→ Write job specifications.

→ Try all free recruitment avenues first.

→ Try doing your own headhunting.

→ If that fails then advertise – in the right place, with the right deal, and using effective design and copy.

→ Prepare thoroughly for interviews.

→ Consider using psychometric tests.

Next steps

What action will you take to apply the information in this chapter? By when will you do it?

_____

_____

_____

_____

If we did all the things we were capable of doing, we would literally astound ourselves.

Thomas Edison

Inspiring commitment

Chapter Five

The importance of reward and recognition

We have already seen how important employees are to you. They are the tools with which you will grow your business. We have looked at how to delegate to them, how to give them the training they need and how to hire more top performers. Before we move on from these internal issues to look at your customers, we are going to focus on the thorny topic of staff motivation.

Why does this matter? Surely if you've gone to all this trouble to hire good people and give everyone all the training they need they ought to be motivated to do the job properly?

To an extent, yes. If you get recruitment, training and job design right, your staff probably will do their jobs perfectly adequately. However, you want them to do more than that. You're growing your business, so you need your staff to do their jobs outstandingly well. You need them to go the extra mile for every customer, to continually innovate so you stay one step ahead of the competition, to see your business as more than just a place where they come to do a nine-to-five job.

You might be sceptical about whether your staff will ever be that engaged. Believe me, it is possible. I have seen companies that have achieved this, and the impact on the growth of that firm and its bottom line is phenomenal.

Think of a sports team. It might have signed the best players and brought in the best coaches, but if it lacks that spark of leadership and motivation, then it will fail to be all it could be.

A large part of your job as managing director is to provide that leadership and motivation. You probably already know how difficult this can be. Motivating your staff with the right mix of salary and benefits is a tricky balancing act. Finding out how your staff feel about their jobs and your company is challenging, and communicating with them is always more difficult than it should be. While larger companies can afford to hire human resources experts to set salaries, arrange benefits, hold appraisals and so on, you have to do it yourself.

There is a lot of theory written about human resources. In this chapter we will avoid the complex theories and focus instead on practical advice. This chapter contains seven ideas you can use right now to enhance the motivation and engagement of your staff. By working through them methodically and implementing each in turn, you will go a long way towards creating that committed and dynamic team that is going to help you grow your business.

Gauge the mood in your workplace

The best place to start is by finding out how your employees currently feel about their jobs and the company. You can bring in external consultants to help you run an employee survey, but it is equally possible to run one yourself with very little investment of time or money.

You simply need to ask your employees to fill in a form anonymously. The following are the sort of questions you might want to ask:

→ How happy are you in your job? (1 lowest, 5 highest)

→ What do you like most about working here?

→ What do you like least?

→ What one change would make you more productive?

There are many variations on that theme. The crucial point to bear in mind is that the survey itself is less important than what happens before and afterwards. You need to explain exactly what you are doing, why you are doing it and how the process will work. Make it crystal clear that you want anonymous, honest answers, and that there will be no comeback to anyone from any answers.

Time saver

Consider using an online survey to ensure complete anonymity. Take a look at **www.surveymonkey.com**, where you can create fairly complex surveys in a few minutes, and then view the results online in real-time, for no cost.

You should also be very careful not to raise your employees' expectations too high. State that not everything they want to happen will happen, but that you will be acting on the findings of your research. This follow-up is vital. If you fail to do anything after the survey you will damage morale. However, with proper explanation and appropriate follow-up, an employee survey can be a catalyst to vastly improved morale.

Offer competitive compensation

Many companies make the mistake of thinking that the only way to keep and motivate their staff is to pay them more. Sure, you need to pay a competitive rate, and including an element of performance-related pay is usually a good way to encourage certain behaviour, but it only goes so far. Ultimately it is just a different number in a pay packet. It has very little effect on how engaged or motivated an employee feels.

A far more powerful incentive is benefits. There are many perks to choose from, such as pensions, holidays, private health insurance, company cars, gym membership and mobile phones. By linking these rewards to performance or longevity of employment, you directly encourage certain behaviours, and employees can see a clear link. They receive some-thing much more tangible, something that has a specific benefit to them.

Many entrepreneurs tend to shy away from offering benefits to their staff, seeing them as expensive luxuries. However, if you implement them properly they can more than pay for themselves. Furthermore, you don't have to spend huge amounts on them. You don't have to offer the most expensive benefits. You simply have to offer the benefits that will motivate your staff.

Think now about what would really excite your staff. It might be one of the traditional benefits listed above, or you might go for something more innovative. For example, in a 2008 survey run by *Employee Bene-fits* magazine the most popular perk that people didn't already get was 'duvet days', where employees have a certain number of days a year when they can call in simply because they don't feel like going into work that day.[2]

When choosing benefits you should bear in mind the tax status. For example, if you offer benefits such as a pension scheme, death in service and childcare vouchers, the employee avoids paying National

---

[2] http://www.employeebenefits.co.uk/cgi-bin/item.cgi?id=4276.

Insurance. However, healthcare schemes, company car allowances and suit allowances are taxed as 'benefits in kind', so the cash equivalent would provide the same value to the employee.

This is not to say that you should avoid taxable benefits. If they would motivate your staff, then they are the right ones to use. However, be aware of tax implications, as this may influence how staff feel about them. For more information on some tax breaks in this area, see Chapter Twelve.

Help your staff with their work–life balance

While in the 1980s everyone wanted the company car and the brick-sized mobile phone, in recent years many employees have shunned material benefits in favour of a better work–life balance. You will probably find that a fair proportion of your staff would rather start and finish work earlier two days a week so they can pick up their children from school than to have an expensive gym membership. Under recent legislation parents have the right to request flexible working and you have a duty to consider these requests.

Toolkit

For more information about the law on flexible working, go online to:
http://www.berr.gov.uk/employment/employment-legislation/employment-guidance/page35662.html.

However, work–life balance is more than a legal requirement. If you are able to find ways to help your employees fit work more easily into their lives they will thank you for it. The excellent employee who receives tax-efficient childcare vouchers from you is unlikely to jump ship when a competitor offers a better paid job. You will keep your best staff and encourage improved productivity through lower absenteeism, reduced stress and enhanced morale.

This is not about you fitting the business around the personal lives of your staff. It is simply about finding ways to accommodate your employees' needs in ways that have no adverse effect on the business. In fact, flexibility is a two-way street and you may find that this allows you to improve how you manage your busier and quieter times.

Be flexible with your benefits

Of course, not everyone is going to be excited by work–life balance improvements. Many of your staff probably do want that expensive gym membership. The key is to recognise that they are all different, that they are all motivated in different ways, so you need to be flexible in how you reward them.

Generally speaking, people in their twenties tend to be more concerned with security of salary and the amount of money coming into the bank every month. Once people reach their thirties and forties they begin to think more long term about pensions, healthcare and other benefits.

How to Grow Your Business for Entrepreneurs

The quickest and most effective way of finding out which benefits your employees really want is simply to ask them. Once you've had some initial thoughts around the benefits you might offer and the results or behaviour you want to reward, you need to meet with all the people you manage to explain that you are considering introducing this scheme, and then ask them what benefits would appeal to them.

Keep your staff informed

If you have reached the point of agreeing a package of benefits with each employee that meets their individual needs, compares well with the competition and is linked to your overall business goals, then you are well on the way to building a loyal and committed workforce. The work you have done so far will make a significant difference to the growth of your organisation over the next 12 months.

However, there is more you need to do. A frequent problem with providing flexible benefits is that employees can become jealous of what they perceive as inequalities in the reward system. It is vital that you are aware of this and communicate with your team to explain how the new system works.

If you give everyone a company mobile phone, it might not be what everyone wants or be particularly motivational to the majority of your staff, but at least everyone knows they're getting the same as everyone else. However, if someone starts leaving at four every day their colleagues can become jealous. It won't matter that the employee arrives at eight and has accepted a 50 per cent cut in holiday allowance. Their colleagues won't think about whether that person is receiving the pension contributions, car allowance or other benefits they do. They'll simply see someone leaving the office at four and will start to resent that colleague.

If left to fester, this resentment can be highly damaging to your company's productivity. At best it will demotivate the employees who feel resentful, reducing their productivity. At worst it will spill over to other employees, making them less productive and possibly even causing some of them to leave the organisation. In every case, these negative feelings diminish the effectiveness of the original benefits. It is therefore important that you address the issue.

The key is frequent, transparent communication. Explain clearly to everyone in your organisation that you are operating a scheme of flexible benefits. Everyone will have different benefits, and if some benefits are linked to performance, some employees may receive more benefits than others. However, everyone is on a level playing field. Make it clear that your door is always open for anyone who wants to discuss the benefits they are receiving.

Danger!

You could consider writing an employees' guide to your benefits packages. However, be careful not to rely on it or to assume that everyone will read it. Written information can be a useful support for verbal communication but should never replace it. Ultimately, having made this investment in staff benefits you need to take every opportunity to remind your staff about them.

Show staff their future

Providing a well-communicated, personalised and competitive package of salary and benefits is one of the most effective ways of attracting, motivating and retaining staff. It is not however *the* most effective way. In the *Employee Benefits* survey mentioned on page 72, the most important factor impacting on employee engagement with the employer, according to 69 per cent of respondents, was simply 'doing interesting work'.

This is not always easy to arrange. Often you need people to do the mundane but essential jobs. You can, though, make them interested in their work by showing them their future. Show employees a vision of where your business is going and how their role will become more exciting as the company grows. Suddenly employees are thinking less about the tedium of the day-to-day grind and more about your shared vision of the future.

Give your staff clear objectives. Run a structured appraisal system in which you regularly assess performance against those objectives, agree future objectives and discuss skills and career development. Do this for every employee, even the most junior. Enthusiasm is infectious, and if you can make every single member of your team excited about your growing business, the enthusiasm will spread so that before long your staff have become much, much more than the sum of their individual parts.

Money matters, but what really attracts people to a job and what keeps them there is the quality of management and the existence of achievable and worthwhile goals. Offer them those and you'll never look back.

Give something back to the community

The final piece in the motivation jigsaw is looking beyond your organisation at the wider community. People want to do work they find interesting, and they want to be properly rewarded for their achievements, but they also want to work for an organisation that does more than just make profits for its owners. Forward-thinking employers are discovering that they can vastly improve employee motivation with a relatively minor investment in community projects.

This might take the form of donating a percentage of profits to a local animal sanctuary. Or you might give staff a day or two a year to volunteer for a local conservation charity. Or you might all go and spend a day together renovating a local homeless shelter. There will be a cost associated, but the resulting upsurge in commitment to your organisation will more than justify the time and financial expense.

Best of all, there's absolutely no need for you to spend time researching and planning the project. It is infinitely more effective if your staff are in charge of it themselves. Tell them you want to do something along these lines, and then set up a suggestions box, where they can place their ideas, say, over the next month.

Make it clear what sort of time and financial investment you are prepared to make – don't raise expectations that you'll all be spending a fortnight digging a well in Malawi! You can then pick the best suggestion and set up a team who can, in their own time, arrange for it to happen. See Chapter Eight for advice on how you can also use this charitable work to promote your business.

Coming up in Part Three of this book are several chapters on how to build your most important asset – your customers. First, here's a look at a company that offers us several lessons in how to motivate staff.

Case study
The Insert & Leaflet Team

'Although I had run small teams previously I had never run a sales team until I launched TILT in 2004 at the age of 27,' says Ben Allan, managing director of The Insert & Leaflet Team (TILT). 'We started out paying our employees a salary plus commission. I believed this was all the incentive that a salesperson should need to motivate them. In the first year, sales were steady, but not prolific, and we ended up making a loss.'

Allan was, however, convinced he had spotted a gap in the market. TILT publishes *asrecommended*, a consumer guide to financial, retail and mail order products. It is delivered direct to pre-selected consumers and carries editorial from experts and celebrities like chef Antony Worrall Thompson, money-management guru Alvin Hall and *Fifth Gear* presenter Vicki Butler-Henderson. TILT makes its money from selling advertising in these publications.

However, back in 2005 with competition rising and sales flagging, Allan knew he had to change something if he was ever to grow his fledgling business beyond five million copies a year. He looked at how he was rewarding his sales team. He promised that if the team hit a particular sales target then the team member responsible for the sale would win a bottle of champagne. The effect was immediate and startling.

Allan says: 'I was amazed to find that a tangible, short-term incentive lifted call rates by 12 per cent. The monetary value of that reward was just £75 yet it lifted sales rates by £54,000 for that particular publication. At the time it seemed crazy as the financial burden to me was nominal, yet the result was phenomenal. This got me thinking about the possibilities of incentives.'

Following the success of the first challenge, he developed an incentive programme that presented non-financial rewards for meeting call targets. The rewards ranged from vouchers to champagne, to extra days of holiday. Allan reports that the costs didn't tangibly affect the company's bottom line.

He continues: 'That all worked so well that we began offering spa days, Christmas shopping days and the company ski trip. At face value these rewards may seem expensive. Yet compared to the sales yield they're cheap. I even made the programme accessible to the administration team for meeting administration targets focused around payment chasing and general accuracy.'

At times of high pressure, he implements the 'Grand in Your Hand' challenge, where if the team hits the target set then they receive £1,000 in their hand, tax paid. This incentive is reserved purely for tight situations such as severe economic conditions where the company needs to make hundreds of thousands of pounds of sales in a short period of time. Consequently, even this scheme usually costs no more than 1 per cent of the revenue it generates.

This focus on employee motivation has had a stunning impact on TILT. Since 2005 it has grown 200 per cent every year, and in 2008 it produced 62.5 million copies of *asrecommended*, spread across monthly publication of the various sector-based titles. Turnover in 2007 was £6.7 million, with profits in excess of £1 million.

Allan concludes:

> *'Remember that money doesn't motivate everyone. A working environment with tangible rewards and incentives is a more dynamic, fun and productive place to be.'*

Web bonus

At our website, **www.forentrepreneursbooks.com**, click on the 'How to Grow Your Business' button. On the link for Chapter Five you'll read about how Aidan Cook, the managing director of Sense Internet, a Leeds-based new media company, was able to increase employee retention and productivity by giving something back to the community.

Key points

→ Run an employee survey.

→ Make a list of benefits you currently offer and those you think might motivate your staff.

→ Consider what you could do to improve the work–life balance of your staff in a way that doesn't adversely affect the business.

→ Meet all your staff to find out what benefits they would value.

→ Communicate your new benefits system to everyone in your company.

→ Establish a system of regular staff appraisals.

→ Ask your staff to think of ways the company could give back to the community.

Next steps

What action will you take to apply the information in this chapter? By when will you do it?

_____

_____

_____

_____

Growing customers

Part Three

If we don't take care of our customers, someone else will.

Anonymous

The foundation of growth – customer retention

Why customer retention matters

Very often entrepreneurs suffer problems with customer retention. They become so focused on winning new customers that they forget about the ones they have already. They exhaust themselves with the effort of marketing and selling, only to find that revenues remain static – simply because they're losing customers as quickly as they're winning them.

Does this sound familiar? If so, then you need to take action right now. Before you even think about winning any new customers, you need to take steps to secure the ones you already have.

Ultimately, your existing customers are the foundations on which you will grow your business. Your staff and your internal structures are the tools with which you achieve that growth, but before you start increasing your turnover and profits you need to ensure that your foundations are secure.

You might think you don't need to worry about it because you're so good at sales and marketing that you're winning customers more rapidly than you're losing them. Don't fall into this trap. Put simply, if you can't keep your customers you will never achieve ongoing business growth. Here's why:

1 You will almost certainly have a limited pool of customers. No matter how large the pool is, you will eventually burn through it until there's no one left to sell to. That's when your company starts shrinking.

2 Previous customers tend to be more profitable. You know what they want and they trust you to deliver it, so you spend less on customer service.

3 Happy customers will recommend you to their friends, family members and other contacts. This type of word-of-mouth recommendation is vastly more effective and considerably cheaper than any other form of marketing.

4 Dissatisfied customers, on the other hand, drain resources into complaint resolution. Before you know it, you're spending so much time pacifying unhappy customers that you don't have time to deal with new ones, so they rapidly become dissatisfied, and then you have no time to find new customers – and so the circle becomes increasingly 'vicious'.

How to Grow Your Business for Entrepreneurs

5 It costs several times more to acquire a new business customer than it does to sell to an existing one. In fact, there are thousands of businesses that have not needed to find any new customers – they've put all their energies into delighting the ones they already have and have grown significantly as a result.

Even if you already have a loyal customer base, I'd advise you to have a look through this chapter. You may pick up some useful tips on how to make that customer base even more solid.

Keeping customers happy can be hard to do. Even large companies with their enormous resources and state-of-the-art contact centres find it difficult. Just think back to all the times one of them has kept you on hold or has billed you incorrectly, or has made it impossible for you to complain about a faulty product.

If the large companies can't get it right, how are you expected to do so? Well, no matter how stretched you are, by following the advice in this chapter you will be able to make improvements to your customer retention.

What do your customers really think of you?

→ How satisfied are your customers?

→ Why are some dissatisfied?

→ What could you change to make more of them happy with your products or services?

Even if you think you know the answers to these questions, you might be surprised to find out how they really feel.

Much of the investment in customer retention programmes is wasted because the company assumes it knows what its customers want. But the only way to really find out what your customers want is to ask them.

Just as with your employee surveys, you can bring in expensive consultants to run a customer satisfaction survey, or you can follow these steps to carry out your own.

Work out whose opinions you want

Unless you have a very small number of customers or you have considerable resources to devote to your research project, you will not be able to survey all your customers. The more opinions you gather the better your research will be, but this must be offset against the time and expense involved. So aim for a happy compromise, investing just enough to ensure that your sample will be representative.

Once you have decided on your budget and sample size you then need to decide which customers will be in your sample. You can do this simply by thinking about which are the most important. Which ones would cause you the most problems if they were no longer customers? If you have a large number of equally important customers then choose those who are the most representative of the entire group.

Decide the best medium

There are several ways you can contact your customers, and there are pros and cons to each. An online survey, promoted by email, is the cheapest option. There are websites on which you can design professional-looking surveys in a matter of minutes. However, it is only suitable if you have your customers' email addresses and know that those customers have regular internet access.

Postal questionnaires involve print costs, but if you can include the survey in existing correspondence, such as invoices, statements or promotional materials, you can make it a fairly cost-effective solution. Both online and postal research are best suited for simple surveys that will take up little of the respondent's time.

If you want to get more in-depth answers you need to invest in telephone surveys or even face-to-face focus groups. You may find it more difficult to persuade customers to take part, and it will cost more, but, because they allow a two-way conversation, you will end up with more profound insights into customer satisfaction.

Decide what to ask

One of the most important decisions is what to ask your customers. The simplest solution is just to ask them to rate their satisfaction with your product or service. However, that doesn't tend to produce an accurate representation of customer satisfaction.

For one thing, responses can be heavily affected by mood. For another, our satisfaction is not necessarily with the company in question. For example, the satisfaction you feel with your new house might be more to do with the area you've moved into than with the house itself. So, you should spend some time working out what questions you can ask to gain accurate responses.

Consider a simple solution

While many companies prefer to compile complex lists of questions, there is a simpler solution: ask your customers whether they would recommend your product or service. This approach has the virtue of being straightforward, to the point and, most crucially, related to the bottom line.

In his recent book *The Ultimate Question*,[3] research guru Fred Reichheld advocates the use of the Net Promoter Score. Put simply, this is asking customers to rate on a scale from one to ten their willingness to recommend your product or service to a friend or colleague. For the company that wants to get a clear indication of levels of customer satisfaction, it is hard to beat this simple approach.

You might want to consider beginning your research with this question. Would you be able to organise that this week? Then, if your average score is less than seven, you know there are some problems, and you can plan some more in-depth research to identify exactly where the problems lie and what you need to do to improve that score.

Take action

Ultimately, no matter how good the research, it is worthless unless it results in some action. In fact it can be worse than worthless: you raise customer expectations by surveying them, but failure to act on your findings can be detrimental to your business.

However, if you have asked the right questions to the right customers through the right medium, you should now have some

---

[3] http://www.theultimatequestion.com/heultimatequestion/home.asp.

extremely useful information that can help you turn dissatisfied customers into enthusiastic promoters of your business. All you need to do is address their concerns.

Ten ways to keep your customers

Your customer satisfaction survey will give you the best indication of what you need to do to improve your customer retention. However, over the years I have seen countless businesses make radical improvements to their customer retention by implementing one or more of these ten simple and affordable steps.

1 Treat your customers as individuals

The first step to delivering excellent customer service is to ensure you know who your customers are, and to keep a clear record of your relationships with them. For larger businesses, this often means investing millions of pounds in one of the infamous customer relationship management (CRM) systems.

You won't need anything so grand, or expensive. You simply need to set up a centralised record that everyone in your company can access and update. You can buy a simple database like ACT! or you can keep it really simple and just have a spreadsheet on your server.

This customer database should contain contact details of all your customers and a record of all your interactions with them. It should allow any member of your staff to rapidly recognise them and to see the history of the relationship, so enabling them to resolve most issues with a single phone call.

> **Danger!**
>
> It is crucial that you keep your databases up to date and accurate. To do this you will need the buy-in of your staff, so tell them about it, stress its importance and conduct regular checks.

How to Grow Your Business for Entrepreneurs

2 Be easy to deal with

Making your company easy to deal with will encourage customers to come back. It's an obvious fact, but it never ceases to amaze me how many companies are so difficult to deal with. How many sales do you lose every week by not having a salesperson available to give a quote, or by not making a delivery on time, or by making it difficult for a customer to order online?

Set aside a couple of hours in the coming week to do some mystery shopping. Think of all the ways a potential customer could get in touch with your company, and then try to make that contact yourself, as if you were a customer. You may be unpleasantly surprised by how difficult your company is to deal with. Resolve to deal with these difficulties immediately.

3 Surprise them!

Everybody loves getting something for free, so imagine how much your customers would love you if you gave them a free gift. Is there something you could give your customers that would cost you very little but that would surprise them and put a smile on their face?

It could be unused stock, an introduction to one of your other customers or a free critique of their website. Ask your staff for suggestions. Mull it over. Surprise someone like this and you could make them a customer for life.

4 Communicate with your customers

No matter what the problem – whether it's with your products, your employees or anything else – if your lines of communication with your customers are open you will, in most cases, be able to resolve it and keep the customer. You lose customers when they see your company as a faceless provider of a product or a service.

Make it difficult for customers to stop buying from you by showing them that you are a real person. Go out and visit your most important customers or speak to them when they come into your premises. Get to know them. Let them get to know you. When you run out of time for the face-to-face interaction, phone or email the others.

Do everything you possibly can to let them know that you are always available for them to discuss any concerns. Then ensure that you fulfil that promise. Never hide from your customers, no matter how badly wrong things might have gone. Talk to them, explain what went wrong and what you're doing to fix it – you may find them more understanding than you expect.

5 Focus on key dates

While you can get something wrong at any point and lose a customer, there are key dates in every customer relationship – both business and consumer. They might be subscription renewals or review meetings. Think about when your customer relationships are at their most vulnerable and put in place a plan for pre-empting approaches from your competitors.

You could ensure you step up your service levels at that time or give your customers a financial incentive to stay loyal to you, or simply pick up the phone and ask them how things are going. However, be careful not to deliver a good service only at these key dates – your customers will rumble you very quickly.

6 Become irreplaceable

In general, client retention focuses on making the customer *want* to keep buying from you, but you may be able to take it a step further and ensure that your customer *needs* to keep buying from you. Think about ways of enmeshing your products and services so profoundly in your customer's life or operations that they will find it almost impossible to do without you.

A good example of this is software that underpins every application the customer runs. Technically the customer could change software provider, but it could involve changing every single application they use, and most buyers would be keen to avoid the hassle.

At the very least you should strive to provide your customers with benefits that they simply can't get anywhere else. You already know them better than your competitors, so you're ideally placed to give them exactly what they need. Use that advantage before you lose it.

7 Under-promise and over-deliver

When a customer asks for something, work out when you can deliver it, how much you will need to charge and what quality it will be. Tell them you will do it slightly more slowly than that, at a marginally higher price and at fractionally lower quality. Then, when you deliver according to your original plan, your customer will be delighted that you've done it more rapidly and cheaply and to a higher standard than expected.

You've not disappointed your customer by failing to deliver on an optimistic promise. You've not even just satisfied them by delivering on a realistic promise. You've genuinely impressed them by appearing to go the extra mile for them. They'll leave with a smile. They'll be back. And they'll probably bring their friends with them.

8 Build a culture of customer service

In the rush to grow it can be very easy to develop a culture in your organisation that prioritises customer acquisition over retention. New customers are by and large more exciting than the ones we've had for years. Almost without knowing it, we focus our energies on those new customers to the detriment of the ones who have been loyal for years and helped get our business off the ground.

Invest time in creating a culture that values retention as highly as acquisition. You can do this by sharing with your staff the points made at the start of this chapter on why retention matters. You can do it by providing regular updates on how well they're keeping customers. You can do it by offering financial incentives for customer retention. However you do it, you need to make sure that everyone is working together to build these solid foundations for growth.

9 Encourage complaints

A common mistake is to assume that because no customers have complained they are all satisfied. In the UK we have an in-built aversion to complaining. Even when profoundly dissatisfied we tend not to complain – we just take our business elsewhere. How many customers have you had who never complained about anything you did but just quietly stopped using you?

Give customers every opportunity to complain. Actively encourage it. Don't see it as a personal criticism. See it as valuable feedback that you can use to improve your business. In fact, you will find that if you welcome complaints and properly handle grievances, you will turn complaining customers into your most loyal customers.

10 Get rid of some customers

It might seem an odd question in a chapter about customer retention, but do you really want all your customers? Take a look at your customer base. Is there one customer that takes up far more of your company's resources than they pay for? Is there one that, no matter how well you do your job, always complains? Is there one that's always late paying bills? Is there one that is just incredibly expensive to deliver to?

When you're starting out you need to keep hold of every single customer you can, but now you're more established you might find it pays to phase out these unprofitable customers. It will enable you to devote more time to profitable customers and to finding new ones. In the next chapter there is much more advice on how to identify customers you don't want and how to get rid of them. We also start looking at how to find new customers.

If you could implement just one of these ten strategies a month, every month, over the next year, imagine what that would do for your customer retention, and therefore your turnover. In the next chapter you'll discover how you can make marketing investments that really work. First, here is the story of how one company mastered the challenges of customer retention.

Case study
Pimlico Plumbers

Pimlico Plumbers was established in 1979 in the basement of an estate agent's offices. It grew well in the early years and hit £1 million turnover by 1986. However, growth levelled off at around that point for many years. Looking back, MD Charlie

Mullins believes this was caused partly by the difficult trading conditions of the early 1990s recession and partly by a lack of focus on customer retention.

'We weren't keeping enough of our customers,' he says. 'We'd always been good at the plumbing side of it, and we could sort out people's problems, but we were letting ourselves down on the customer service side.'

It is a problem many, if not most, plumbers face. However, few are astute enough to recognise it, and only a tiny fraction are able to do anything about it. Mullins and his team at Pimlico Plumbers are in that tiny fraction, and their resulting success is a vivid demonstration of the power of customer service.

He says: 'There are too many cowboys in this industry, too many rude, rip-off merchants who turn up late in rusty vans with their backsides hanging out of their trousers. We completely reject this way of doing business. Pimlico Plumbers wear clean uniforms, they turn up on time in spotless vans and they all carry company ID.'

The company operates a 24-hour, 365-day call centre, which is operated by staff who can relate to customers. 'To be frank,' says Mullins, 'in the past we employed too many call centre staff who were just downright rude. Unsurprisingly it drove away customers. Now we only hire people who will take the time and trouble to understand a customer's situation.'

In emergencies Pimlico will get a plumber out within the hour, regardless of whether it is night or day. All customers are made aware of all charges before work begins and there is a clear breakdown of costs available on the company's website.

None of this has been easy to achieve and it has taken many years. However, it has produced results. Today, more than 80 per cent of the 1,200 to 1,400 jobs Pimlico completes every week are for returning customers. The company's turnover exceeded £10 million in 2006, and in 2008 Mullins expects it to reach £15 million.

'We're not perfect,' says Mullins. 'I wish we were but there's always something to improve. We're looking to expand out to the M25, but we will only do it very steadily, always maintaining our levels of customer service.'

He concludes with this advice on keeping customers:

'Be transparent with everything, especially your charges. Employ the best people. Make sure your customers understand your business and your customers. Most of all keep it simple. Everything we've done is just common sense. The problem is that common sense ain't that common!'

Key points

→ Customer retention is a prerequisite for business growth.

→ Begin by finding out what your customers really think of you.

→ Treat your customers as individuals.

→ Be easy to deal with.

→ Give your customers something for free.

→ Communicate with your customers.

→ Focus on key dates in the buying cycle.

→ Make yourself irreplaceable.

→ Under-promise and over-deliver.

→ Build a culture of customer service.

→ Encourage complaints.

→ Get rid of some customers.

Next steps

What action will you take to apply the information in this chapter? By
when will you do it?

_____

_____

_____

_____

Half the money I spend on advertising is wasted; the trouble is I don't know which half.

John Wanamaker

Marketing investments that work

Chapter Seven

No more waiting for the phone to ring

Marketing is one of the most important ways to grow a business. The problem is that it can be very expensive. If you're serious about growing your business, you will almost certainly need to invest some money in marketing. The trick is to invest wisely.

First of all we're going to make sure you aim your marketing at the right people. After all, you can produce the best marketing campaign the world has ever seen – with ground-breaking creative imagery, compelling copy, brilliantly innovative use of media space – but if it brings you the wrong sort of customers it's a waste of time and money.

The wrong sort of customers? Surely there's no such thing as the wrong sort of customer? You're not going to turn away anyone who offers to pay you good money, are you?

No, of course you're not going to. If someone walks into your shop, calls your sales team or finds some other way of approaching you and offering you good money to deliver products or services, you almost certainly aren't going to turn them down, although it does happen. I once knew a graphic design agency that advertised on its website for clients. Rather arrogantly the agency claimed it was so good that it had space for only one more client and so potential clients were going to have to pitch for the opportunity to hire them. I wasn't altogether surprised when within six months the agency was in administration.

No, I'm not advocating that sort of arrogance, though I am going to show you how to be more targeted with your marketing.

When you're starting out you tend to sell to people who know you, people you've worked for in the past or who have been recommended by kind friends and family. That's great – you need to do that to get going. However, you're now up and running, and this book is all about how to progress to the next stage.

So, you need to start focusing on the people who are most likely to be your best customers. Rather than waiting for business to walk in through the door, and then getting your head down to deliver whatever is required, you're going to go out and find exactly the customer you want and you're going to do the work for them that you want to do.

It'll take a while. It will involve brave decisions – some of which might be to turn away the wrong sort of customers, even to stop working with long-standing clients. But in the end, you will have transformed your business into one that has a growing number of highly profitable customers, is doing work you and your staff enjoy and, perhaps most valuable of all, has a burgeoning brand.

What are you selling?

At the heart of every good marketing campaign is a clear message. If you want your investment in marketing to pay off you need to develop a clear and appealing message that will resonate with your potential customers.

You might think you already know what that message is.

You're probably wrong. This is because your marketing message so far has been aimed at those existing contacts you needed to get you up and running. How they view you and your company will inevitably be very different from how someone who doesn't know you at all will view you. So, now is a good time to revisit your core proposition, to look again at the message you're taking to the market.

In Chapter One you conducted your SWOT analysis, so you have a good idea of where your own company fits into the market and the opportunities that it can exploit through its strengths. Your marketing message should be based on those findings, but they should always be expressed in terms of the benefit to your customer.

Instead of talking about the new technology you've invented, you should always talk about how it makes people's lives easier. Instead of talking about how your staff are the most experienced in the market, you should talk about how they can provide their clients with unparalleled insights.

Time saver

A useful phrase when going through this process is, 'So what?' Whenever you think you've identified the benefit of your product or service to your customers, ask yourself, 'So what?' Do it enough times and you'll soon get to the core of what it is you're selling, and why your customers want to buy it from you. This is your marketing message.

Pinpointing your ideal customers

You probably think you know who your best customers are, but before you spend money on a marketing campaign aimed at attracting more like them, try this simple exercise that will help you find out whether or not you're right.

Begin by listing all your customers. If you have only a handful this will be easy. If you have thousands it will be impossible, so instead take a representative sample. Perhaps for three days pick out one customer every two hours who walks into your premises. That should give you 12 customers to consider.

Then, over the next week or two, for each customer work out the following:

1 How much money they spend with you.

2 How much it costs to produce what they buy – remember to factor in staff costs as well as raw materials, hardware and so on.

3 How much it costs to service the relationship.

4 How much marketing investment it takes to acquire them.

5 How quickly they pay their bills.

6 How much you and your staff enjoy working with them.

Once you have all this data you'll be able to do a rough calculation of who your best customers are. You can work out profitability by subtracting 2, 3 and 4 from 1, and you can factor in desirability with 5 and 6.

Ultimately you don't want any customers where you don't make any profit. However, you might choose to prioritise less profitable customers if they help with your cash flow by being rapid, reliable payers or if you and your staff like working with them because they're good to deal with or they allow you to do work you enjoy.

This is only a rough calculation, but those are the fundamentals of how to work out who your best customers are. By spending a few hours looking at this in just a little more depth, by getting it down on paper, you might be surprised by the results. You might find that a customer you've had for years and always enjoyed working with is actually costing you money. What's the point of you losing money on a customer? You are in effect paying them to use your service or product!

How to Grow Your Business for Entrepreneurs

Or you might find that the customer you and everyone else in your workplace always complains about, and who always pays their bill late, is actually the most profitable one. It may even be that this customer is the one whose profitable business is subsidising all the others you have so much fun working for.

It may be that you put a higher premium on prompt payment or friendly relationships than on profit. That is your prerogative as the one running your company. All this process should do is help you to understand who your best customers are. Maybe this would be a good time to revisit Chapter Six to try to ensure you're doing everything possible to keep those customers. We can then look at how to find more customers like those best ones.

Customer profiling

" **Life is divided into three terms – that which was, which is, and which will be. Let us learn from the past to profit by the present, and from the present to live better in the future.** WILLIAM WORDSWORTH

Once you have compiled the list of your best customers you need to work out what characteristics they tend to have in common. If they are consumers, you might want to ask the following questions:

→ What age are they?
→ Are they mostly male or female?
→ Are they from a particular geographical region?
→ Are they well-off or not?
→ Are they buying one particular type of service or product?

If it's businesses you're selling to, these are the questions to consider:

→ Do they tend to be large or small businesses? How are you defining large and small? Can you put a figure on it?

→ Are they from a particular geographical region?

→ Are they in a certain sector or industry?

→ Are they buying one particular type of service or product?

For business-to-business (B2B) firms it can be easy to slip into the assumption that you're selling just to a company. That is of course true, but you're also selling to people within those companies. Think about the person who buys from you:

→ What is their job title?

→ What age are they?

→ Are they mostly male or female?

→ Are they from a particular geographical region?

By doing all this, you are slowly building a profile of your ideal customers. Bear in mind that not all your perfect customers will fit all these criteria – you're just looking to identify general tendencies, so you can start looking for people who share the same characteristics.

By far the best way of getting all this information is to ask your customers. You can get precise answers to all the questions above and even factor in more specific ones, such as what newspapers they read, what cars they drive and so on, all of which might reveal the characteristics of your ideal customer.

It will take time, but by doing this you will be enhancing the customer database you began building in Chapter Six. This will not only improve your customer service and retention, but it will also form the foundation of your marketing database.

The fundamentals of managing marketing data

There's little point to building up all this data if you're not going to capture it and use it. Whether you use a simple spreadsheet or invest in a more complex marketing database, you should follow these rules on database management.

Obey the law

Since the Data Protection Act became legislation in 1998, there have been strict rules governing the collection, storage and use of data in the UK. Many people who are new to data management assume that the rules are complicated and so ignore them. In so doing they are running the risk of personal and corporate prosecution.

Each situation is different and so it is always wise to obtain legal advice, but broadly speaking there are just four areas in which you need to be careful when it comes to data protection:

1 Gain consent to use new data for specific purposes and then only use it for those purposes.

2 Don't use data in an electronic marketing campaign unless you have complied with e-privacy regulations. These require prior opt-in in some circumstances and opt-out in others. You should also check data against the Telephone and Fax Preference Services.

3 Don't keep data for longer than is necessary to fulfil the purpose for which it was collected.

4 Do not provide personal data to third parties for processing on your behalf without obtaining commitments from them that they will comply with your processing instructions, especially in relation to disclosure and security.

See Chapter Thirteen for further advice from a lawyer on how to comply with the Data Protection Act.

Keep it clean

Keeping your data clean is certainly important. It is also very hard work. However, that can be minimised through organising your data well, by knowing what you have and where you have it. Ensure there is a system for staff to enter customer and prospect data, completing certain fields such as name, job title, phone number and email address.

Data decays at a frighteningly rapid rate and must be continually maintained. If you relax and assume that your data will clean itself, then very quickly you will find that your direct marketing campaigns have become less effective and your reputation among existing and potential customers is beginning to decline.

B2B data is subject to an annual 22 per cent decay rate purely due to staff turnover. That is just those contacts who leave their jobs. When you consider how many people take maternity leave, move to new jobs within companies, relocate overseas and so on, it is not surprising that many people find their B2B data decaying by up to 40 per cent each year.

Create a culture of data protection

Every company needs to have one person who is responsible for the data. However, that person ought to be supported by a culture within which data is important. In too many companies data is seen as someone else's job.

Treat data as your most valuable business asset. Control access to it. Make sure everyone understands its worth. Create business goals and objectives around it. Whatever you do, don't allow everyone to assume it is someone else's responsibility, or just let it grow without an ongoing maintenance plan. It should be treated as a key business asset at board level.

Creating ads that work

By following this process you will soon find that you have a database full of information about your best customers. You will know what it is about them that makes them your best customers and you will be aware of certain characteristics they share.

The really great news is that you can now go out and find more people like them. You can make a well-targeted marketing investment. You can do this by buying advertising space in print or online or by buying lists of prospective customers.

Media owners, whether of your local paper, an industry publication or a website with a global reach, should be able to provide you with a fairly detailed description of their readership, so you'll know whether or not your advertising will reach people you want to do business with.

The sobering news is that you're probably going to have to spend some money to do this. Advertising is not cheap, but it can be very effective if done well. In Chapter Four we looked at how to create successful recruitment ads. The advice applies equally to creating customer ads. I have only two pieces of further advice:

1   Remember the marketing message that you identified earlier in this chapter. Your ad must convey that message to your prospects. When creating your ad, put yourself in their shoes and think how they will receive it. If possible, run it past some of your ideal customers to get their feedback.

2   Bear in mind that advertising is a long-term strategy. It will not produce immediate results. Placing one ad and waiting for the phone to ring is a complete waste of time. You need to run a series of ads over time, and ideally support it with direct mail and other promotional and online techniques.

Do all this and before long you will be reaping the benefits of your investment in advertising.

Creating mailshots that work

While advertising is a long-term marketing tactic, direct mail tends to be more successful at creating short-term results. It is a great way of placing a specific message in front of an individual, and you can very easily track and measure response. Get it right and you'll provide an instant boost to your sales.

However, direct mail can easily become junk mail. Think about what you do with the mailshots that come through your letterbox. What do you do with most of them? If you're anything like me you probably put most straight in the bin, but stop to look at the occasional one, and very occasionally you call the company, look it up online or go and visit the shop.

Think about what causes you to look more closely at the occasional mailshot. What is it about that one that piques your interest? It is almost certainly that it is relevant to you. It is related to an interest you have, whether that is selling your house, reading about triathlons, finding a restaurant for dinner on Saturday night or something else.

Therefore, the key to the success of your direct mail is making it relevant to the recipient. Very few companies get this right. Think about the pile of irrelevant flyers and letters that arrive in your letterbox every day and you'll see just how many companies are wasting money on their direct mail.

Sure, they may be getting some sort of response from these large-scale, untargeted mailings. Maybe they get 1 per cent, perhaps 2 per cent, of recipients responding, but how much does it cost them to generate that business? When you consider the cost of designing the mailer, printing it and delivering it, the margin created by even a 2 per cent response is unlikely to be exciting.

Furthermore, they are damaging their reputation. I can think of at least two companies that constantly send me irrelevant direct mail. I will never buy anything from them, simply because they've irritated me so much. How many other potential customers have they put off like this?

Finally, there is the environmental impact of all this material that is printed, delivered and then binned without so much as a glance. You don't want to be responsible for tonnes and tonnes of paper pointlessly filling our landfill sites.

In this chapter you have already done much of the work necessary to produce well-targeted mailshots.

You have developed a good understanding of your target audience and you have set up a marketing database to capture information about them. You'll keep it up to date, so you're sending your mailshots to the right address, with the right names, and job titles where relevant. You've also profiled your customer base to build a clear picture of the characteristics of your potential new customers, so when you need to add new prospects to your database you can buy lists of only relevant prospects.

You also know why people buy from you, because you've clarified your marketing message. You know what benefits you offer your prospects. So, when you come to design and write your mailshots, you can emphasise that, and make it immediately clear to your recipients that what you're selling is in fact relevant to them.

You're not going to produce a flyer that looks like every other piece of direct mail. You're going to design a mailshot that captures your recipients' attention and that they genuinely want to read.

Finally, because you're running an intelligent direct mail campaign, you're not just going to keep pumping out mailer after mailer, accepting a low and diminishing return. You're going to track the results of each campaign. You're going to test different messages to different audiences. You're going to learn from each mailing that you do, so that every time you invest in a mailshot it's more effective than the last.

Do all of this well and your mailers will stand head and shoulders above the rest of the dross. It will take time, effort and financial investment, but it will be well worth it.

If you're wondering whether there are inexpensive alternatives for marketing your product or service, you'll be encountering 21 of them in the next chapter. First, let's have a look at a company that has made masterful use of marketing to land the clients it really wanted to work with.

Case study
Holler

Will Pyne set up his own company when he was 23. Both he and his partner, James Kirkham, had spent a couple of years after university doing some freelance e-marketing work for record labels, including Sony, Universal and BMG, and in 2003 they decided to formalise the arrangement and set up Holler.

It went well. Clients loved the e-cards the agency produced and began to ask them to produce websites for them. Turnover grew steadily from £208,000 in 2003 to £326,000 in 2004. By 2005 the company was turning over £558,000, and had a solid client base, 90 per cent of which was record labels.

However, Pyne and Kirkham still felt they could achieve more. Pyne says: 'Most of the people we were working for were very set in their ways creatively. We were just churning out the same old stuff and it was stunting our growth. We started thinking that there must be more interesting work out there. Also, we weren't making a lot of profit, because record labels tend to spend all their money on artists rather than online designers like us.'

The pair made a brave decision to swap all their existing clients for more forward-thinking clients who met the twin criteria of wanting exciting, creative design and having money to spend on it. The transition has been far from easy, but in 2008 Holler has achieved it and has transformed itself.

At the start they were lucky, as Pyne recalls: 'One of the guys we'd worked with at a record label had moved to Channel 4 Music, so we got on to a pitch list there. We were a small agency of only about a dozen people up against some of the biggest players in the industry, but they were bowled over by our enthusiasm and the quality of our work, and we got the job.'

Pyne and Kirkham drew up a hit list of premium brands they wanted to work with, like Procter & Gamble and Selfridges. They also changed their branding to change the perception clients had of them as being a small bunch of designers doing stuff for fun, to an established agency that can create innovative campaigns for brave and forward-thinking clients. Finally, Holler hired people with the right experience – heavyweights who would impress the sort of clients the agency wanted on its books.

Perhaps the most difficult decision was ditching clients that didn't fit the new profile. Pyne says: 'We tried to do it gradually by turning down bits and pieces of work, and we found that most accepted the fact that we were evolving. However, we have had to get rid of a couple that didn't share our ambition and were holding us back. It was difficult to do, but failure to do it would have severely limited our growth.'

That growth has been impressive since making those tough decisions. The agency now works for clients like Procter & Gamble and ABN Amro, producing work that the team finds more challenging and interesting. That team has doubled in size to 30. Turnover rose to £840,000 in 2006, £1.57 million in 2007 and £3.2 million in 2008. Most startlingly, the profit margin has multiplied by 50 times, growing from £25,000 in 2005 to £1.25 million in 2008.

Pyne concludes: 'If we hadn't made the changes we did, I believe we would have continued to grow very, very slowly. We would have gone from £30k profit, to £60k, £80k and so on year after year. Making these changes has not only helped us grow, it has transformed our profile and that in turn continues to generate more business.'

He offers this advice to other growing businesses:

'Take the time to work out who will pay a premium for your services. Find customers that will raise your profile. For example, everyone assumes that if the likes of ABN Amro, Procter & Gamble are using Holler, Holler must be good. Finally, remember that running a business is about taking calculated risks. Ditching our original client base and replacing them took confidence and was certainly risky. But it's paid off.'

How to Grow Your Business for Entrepreneurs

Key points

→ Know your core selling points.

→ Work out who your best customers are.

→ Find more like them.

→ Build and maintain a marketing database.

→ Produce advertising that works.

→ Produce direct mail that works.

Next steps

What action will you take to apply the information in this chapter? By
when will you do it?

_____

_____

_____

_____

The secret to creativity is knowing how to hide your sources.

Albert Einstein

21 ways to promote your business on a budget

Chapter Eight

Stop spending – start thinking!

Growing businesses like yours tend not to have large marketing budgets. However, there is much you can do that costs almost nothing. This chapter contains 21 promotional ideas that will cost you very little other than your time.

You're probably acutely aware of the fact that your time is as limited as your marketing budget, so you need to choose where to invest it just as carefully.

Read through all of the 21 ideas, then pick the *one* idea that you believe will have the maximum impact on your sales for the least investment of your time. Then do just that.

Once you've made that one idea work, keep doing it, but come back to the list and pick out the next best idea. It's always better to start off with one straightforward initiative that will work, rather than launching into a raft of complicated ones, which will probably just end up demoralising you and your team.

Time saver

Set up a marketing ideas file. Whenever you have a great idea for how to market your business, write it down and put it in the file. Encourage your staff to do the same. Then once a month go through the file. Before you know it you'll have many, many more than 21 promotional ideas!

> There is no such thing as bad publicity except your own obituary. BRENDAN BEHAN

1 Get to know your media

Ironically, public relations (PR) has got itself a bad reputation. Somehow, the industry has become confused in the popular consciousness with characters like those from the television programme *Absolutely*

Fabulous – self-absorbed clothes horses, who charge vast sums of money and produce little benefit other than to Bollinger's sales figures.

You should not make the mistake of believing that's all there is to public relations. PR is in fact probably *the* most cost-effective way for you to promote your business. Done correctly it is free advertising. In fact it is more powerful than advertising, because rather than you telling potential customers about how great your products and services are, you're getting a third party – a journalist – to do it. A recommendation, even a mention, by an impartial, respected journalist, whether it's in print, on radio or television, carries great weight. Negative comments can destroy brands; positive comments can create millionaires overnight.

That's why large companies spend hundreds of thousands of pounds on PR departments and consultants. You don't need to do that. You can do your own PR relatively simply.

The first step is to get to know your media. From Chapter Seven you already know who you want to reach with your marketing messages. If you have an advertising budget you may even know which media they read, listen to and watch. You now need to find out who the journalists are within those media.

Look online, phone the reception – however you do it, get hold of the names, phone numbers and email addresses of those journalists. It'll be much easier than you think. Bear in mind that trade press or local media want to hear from businesses in their industry or area. Even the national media relies on the PR industry for much of its content.

Once you have these contact details you have the beginnings of a media database. Keep a record of these people and all your interactions with them. Start by emailing them to introduce yourself and your business. Explain simply who you are, what you do and how you can be of use to them.

All newspapers, magazines, television stations and radio stations need people with interesting opinions. Your aim is to become the person they go to on your particular subject. If possible, arrange to meet up – many journalists are amenable to an offer of lunch – and demonstrate how interesting your opinions are. Make it easy for them to contact you for a last-minute quote or interview slot, and when they do call be ready to drop everything.

2 Write press releases

You'll probably find it easy to get hold of the journalists on a local commercial newspaper or an advertising-led trade newsletter. But while these are a good place to start, your goal should really be to reach the more elusive journalists – the ones that people read, listen to or watch, and whose opinions they genuinely respect.

Bear in mind that many of your competitors are already trying to get the attention of those same journalists. That's why you're always reading about those competitors. Well, soon your competitors are going to be reading about you, because you're going to grab the attention of those journalists with a series of press releases.

It is important that you produce a series. Just like advertising, PR doesn't work as a one-off. You need to become recognised over time as a player in a market, as an expert on a subject, as an interesting, reliable and media-friendly commentator.

There is a vast array of topics you can cover in your press releases – below is a list of possible ideas. The golden rule with choosing your subjects is to consider what is going to interest the readers of the publications where you want your press release to be used. Many companies commit the cardinal sin in their press releases of concentrating solely on what the company is doing. Journalists aren't interested in your news – they're interested in what it all means for their readers. So try to get inside the head of those readers and think about what your business is doing that will interest them – for example:

→ hiring new staff;

→ opening new premises;

→ moving into new markets;

→ acquiring new customers;

→ introducing a new product;

→ celebrating an anniversary;

→ taking a position on an industry or local issue;

→ commenting on a new trend;

→ winning an award;

How to Grow Your Business for Entrepreneurs

→ achieving impressive growth;

→ announcing an event.

When writing your press release, always keep in mind why the journalist will be interested in this story. Try to give as much specific detail as possible, keep the language clear and simple, avoid jargon and double-check for basic errors in spelling, grammar and facts.

Send your press release in the body of an email, with an enticing subject line that will encourage the journalist to open and read it. Then follow up with a phone call after a couple of days to check it arrived and to ask whether it was of any interest. If you've chosen your subject well and written it engagingly, you may be surprised how keen the journalist is to use your press release, or at the very least to contact you soon afterwards for comment on a subject.

3 Get hold of editorial schedules

Most media outlets produce an editorial calendar, very often far in advance. It details what subjects it will be covering on that day or in that issue. You should be able to obtain these, just by asking your journalist contacts or even their administrative support. It will allow you to tailor your press releases to the subjects that are being covered at that time.

4 Support a charity

If you find that journalists aren't picking up your press releases or writing about you, you need to work harder to get noticed. A great way to do this is to associate yourself with a charity.

Journalists are a fairly sceptical bunch, and they'll know perfectly well that you're trying to get them to publicise your business for free. If you start donating to a local charity or giving staff time off to volunteer for good causes, and then start publicising it, those journalists will still know what you're up to. However, if you're doing something of interest to their readers, they'll want to write about it.

They key is not to do it cynically. You're doing it because you want to sell more – that's what businesses do. But pick a charity with which your business has a genuine affinity. Are there homeless people outside your shops? Consider allowing two members of staff an afternoon every month to volunteer at a local shelter. Do you manufacture children's toys? Consider taking the whole team out for two days to help build a local playground.

The closer you can link your philanthropy to the genuine concerns of your business the more effective it will be, not just as a public relations tool, but also as a way of bringing your staff together in a common cause, of feeling that their jobs are more than just ways of making money.

Tell journalists what you're doing, explain why the cause matters to you. Invite them to come and see the effects of the partnership on the charity and your business.

Most important of all, make it a long-term relationship. If you're not immediately rewarded with a flurry of publicity, don't pack it in, leaving the charity short of funds or volunteers. See it through for the long term. Eventually journalists and readers will take notice of a business that has quietly helped a charity for several years without recognition.

5 Run a competition

The media loves running competitions. It encourages people to buy their publications or tune into their shows. If you can devise a clever, innovative competition with a prize that people will want, then you should be able to find a media outlet willing to publicise it for you.

6 Create a stunt

It was way back in 1999 that *FHM* projected the image of a naked Gail Porter on to the Houses of Parliament. It generated a huge amount of publicity, sales soared. You might not want to go that far, but there will be a stunt you could run to generate media coverage for your business.

Whatever stunt you come up with, make sure that it conveys the selling points and business benefits of your product or service. Ideally integrate your innovative stunt into your other marketing activity, so it uses your company branding, and maybe reinforces a message in your advertising and direct marketing. You should also carefully consider any legal or health and safety restrictions.

7 Real-life product placement

Large brands spend millions of pounds placing their products in films and television programmes. The idea is that if we see Daniel Craig or Sienna Miller enjoying a product, we'll want to emulate them and will go out and buy the product. It's clearly an idea that works – those big brands wouldn't spend so much on it if it didn't.

Unless you're especially well connected you're not going to be able to persuade Daniel Craig or Sienna Miller to endorse your products. However, you can still get your products out there. Why not hand out samples to passers-by or give them free to be used in smart local bars and restaurants? If people see your products in desirable places they're more likely to desire them.

If you're feeling particularly adventurous you could even hire actors to subtly promote your products. They don't have to do it onscreen – they can do it in bars, clubs, restaurants and shops. Place these under-cover marketers in places where you know your ideal customers are likely to be, and have them talk about how great your products are.

Several leading brands do this on university campuses. They pay the opinion leaders at the university to promote their products to their fellow students. They create a word-of-mouth buzz and encourage others to try the product. Why not try it for your product?

8 Partner marketing

How many businesses are there who target the same people as you? Step outside your premises and look up and down your street or go and read the names of the other businesses who share your office block. How many of them already have customers that you want? And don't you have customers that they want?

If you were to partner with one of those businesses and if you recommended each other to your customers, how much would it boost your business? You don't have to make the recommendation too explicit. In fact you should be careful of alienating your existing customers by pushing products or services on to them that they don't want, but if you find the right partners your customers might see it as a desirable service.

For example, if you run a business selling walking holidays in Scotland, would your customers like to know about a great place to buy walking boots? If that shop offered a 10 per cent discount to anyone who had booked through you, might they not see that 10 per cent as a reduction in the cost of the holiday they'd booked with you? And then, what if that boot retailer started popping one of your holiday brochures in the bag with every purchase?

Danger!

The potential of partner marketing is enormous. However, approach it with caution. Ensure that you only partner with companies that will provide as good a service and product as you do. Continually monitor the relationship to ensure that your partner is marketing as vigorously as you are.

9 Networking

Networking is a horrible word. It always makes me think of desperate businesspeople wearing cheap suits and false smiles, making tedious conversation over warm wine in out-of-town hotels. It's also quite a frightening concept. Many entrepreneurs shy away from networking events, not because they're keen to avoid the warm Chardonnay, but because they're nervous about walking into a room full of strangers.

Seventy per cent of success in life is showing up.

WOODY ALLEN

How to Grow Your Business for Entrepreneurs

That fear is perfectly normal. It is an odd and frightening thing to do – at first anyway. However, by following a few simple techniques and having the courage to give it a go, you'll soon be out there enthusiastically networking your way to new business.

It does work. Every day in every town and city across the UK businesspeople meet, chat about what they do and swap business cards, and as a result pick up new customers. The chances are that today, within a 20-minute drive of where you are right now, there will be an event at which you could pick up new customers.

Finding these events is easy. Go online and search for networking events in your area. There is a rapidly growing networking industry and there is probably an event in your area dedicated to bringing businesspeople together for networking. You'll have to pay a small fee to turn up, but this will more than pay for itself.

If there aren't any networking events, then look for an industry event you could go to. Or maybe there's a community event or a local club you could join. Whether or not the people there have gathered for that specific purpose, there will be groups of people to whom you can promote your products and services.

So, how to do this networking thing?

Well, first of all, you're not there to sell. Do not turn up to the event ready to press your company on to people. You'll feel uncomfortable and people will start to avoid you.

Instead, go hoping to find out about the other people. Bear in mind that most other attendees will be as nervous as you. When you arrive, don't assume that they all know each other and you're an outsider. Confidently approach someone standing alone and introduce yourself with a smile and outstretched hand. The smile you see spread across their features will be one of relief that someone friendly has finally spoken to them.

While you talk, remain open with your body language to the rest of the room. Stand together, facing out, allowing others to join your group. As you move around the room, look for groups that are open like this. They want you to join them. They want to find out about you, and probably to sell to you!

Make it your mission to find out as much as you can about everyone in that room. Get to know as much as you can about their businesses, their lives, the challenges they face and what they're trying to achieve in their lives. Ask questions and show interest in the answers.

If you do that successfully, believe me, you will find opportunities to sell your products. You won't need to push them on to anyone. You will have found people who genuinely need what you have to sell.

Of course it isn't easy to do this. It takes courage and practice. Start off with an event this week and just see it as a challenge. What's the worst that could happen? You have an uncomfortable hour or two with people you'll never see again. What's the best that could happen? You could find new customers and boost your sales.

10 Speak at an event

No matter what you sell, there will be an event where you could stand up and speak. It may be an industry conference that your prospective customers attend. Or it might be your village fête, which is packed with potential customers for your local business. Whatever the event, the organisers will probably be crying out for people who are willing to act as speakers.

Most people are terrified of public speaking. If you are one of those lucky few who can do it well, you should jump at every opportunity you get to make your voice heard. Every speaking engagement is a chance to demonstrate your expertise, to show people how likeable you are, possibly even to explain how your product or service can improve their lives.

Toolkit

If you are among the great majority who would rather put pins in their eyes than have to speak in front of an audience, look into joining an organisation such as Toastmasters International. It provides a friendly forum for its members to regularly practise public speaking and has a growing number of clubs across the UK. Online, go to www.toastmasters.org.

How to Grow Your Business for Entrepreneurs

11 Take a stand at a show

Having a stand at a show is a great way of getting your message to a large number of people at one time. Very often attendees are there specifically to see the stands, so you will have an audience that is not only captive, but also extremely attentive. Can you think of shows, exhibitions or other events where many of your potential customers all gather in one place?

There's a trade show for every industry, as well as hundreds of consumer events like the Boat Show and Ideal Home Exhibition. Stands at these events tend to be expensive, but with some inventive negotiation you may be able to get a stand relatively cheaply. Think about what you could offer the organisers in return. Do you have products or services that the organisers need?

Once there, make your stand as open and inviting as possible. Greet passers-by, talk to everyone who shows an interest, capture their contact details and then always follow up after the event.

If you can't afford a stand and can't barter for one, think more laterally about the events. Think about where else you could go to be seen by your prospects. What about university fairs, or on the route between train stations and the local sports stadium on match days?

12 Join a trade association

Many entrepreneurs are reluctant to join trade associations. As go-it-alone pioneers we tend to keep these kind of collective bodies at arm's length, and find it hard to see what membership will do for us other than make us a couple of hundred pounds worse off.

However, if managed correctly, membership of a trade association is a minor investment that can more than pay for itself. The key is to see it as opening up an opportunity that you can exploit. Most trade associations are poor at telling their members about the benefits on offer, and many even fail to do much to bring their members together.

However, if you actively and vigorously exploit all the opportunities, by attending events, using online forums, maybe even writing articles for the newsletter, you may find it a valuable source of new business.

At the very least, it should put you in contact with your peers, many of whom will be a goldmine of ideas for further cost-effective marketing.

13 Copy your competitors

The sincerest form of flattery is imitation, and if your competitors are cleaning up with their brilliant promotional work shouldn't you pay them the compliment of copying them? In most cases there's nothing to stop you doing this, and it can save you a huge amount of time you might otherwise spend trying to reinvent the wheel.

Visit a couple of your competitors, either physically or virtually, and find out what they are doing in their marketing, their product development, their customer service and so on. Pick their best ideas, copy them and do them even better.

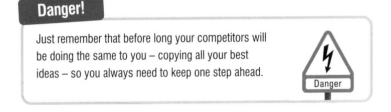

Danger!

Just remember that before long your competitors will be doing the same to you – copying all your best ideas – so you always need to keep one step ahead.

14 Make friends with your competitors

Often we're so caught up in competition that we forget to look for possible areas of mutual benefit. If you're up against a company that is winning a lot of new business, consider making a friendly approach, offering to take care of any overflow work they can't handle. If they're growing that fast, they may not have prepared the resource to deliver it and may be glad to hear from you.

15 Guerrilla marketing

One type of guerrilla marketing activity is piggy-backing your marketing on to another, better-known campaign. This is done most famously by large sportswear brands at events such as the football World Cup, but you can take the idea and apply it to smaller industry and community events.

For example, if there is a major industry conference coming up, you could hold a seminar just before it at a nearby venue, inviting key prospects to get together to discuss an important industry subject that isn't covered by the conference agenda. Or if there is a fun run taking place in a local park, you might want to hand out flyers for your café in the crowd promoting your business, and offer a discount to any competitors after the run.

It can be a superbly inexpensive way of getting your products or services out to a large, engaged audience. Like PR stunts, it can be a risky tactic. Be careful not to infringe any copyrights, and where possible work with the event organiser, so that you are adding value to their event rather than detracting attention from it.

Leo had mixed up guerrilla marketing with gorilla marketing.

16 Answerphone message

Take time to consider every possible interaction a potential customer has with your company. Are you taking every opportunity to market your services? For example, if a prospect calls after hours, is your answerphone message the usual bland, downbeat 'Please leave a message and we'll call you back'? Think about how you could improve it, to make it more likely that that prospect will leave a message and be enthusiastic about hearing from you when you return the call. Consider what you say and how you say it.

17 Paint your car

You would probably be surprised by how little it costs to put your company name, website address, phone number and logo on your car. The technique is known in the industry as car wrapping and you can get it done for as little as £1,000.

You might have some reservations about turning your car into a promotional vehicle, but you might put them aside when you realise just how effective it can be at growing your business.

Unlike traditional advertising, which is only seen by some of the people who read that publication, watch that channel or pass that billboard, advertising on your car moves around with you, so many different people see it. If you want to get your name known in a local area there are few better ways of achieving it.

18 Sell more to existing customers

It can be easy to focus marketing efforts so heavily on finding new customers that you forget your richest seam of potential new sales: your existing customers. They already know how great your products or services are and you already have many ways of informing them about new opportunities to buy from you.

Think about how you could cross-sell whenever you speak to customers. However, be careful not to appear pushy. We all know the call centres, banks and other organisations that you can't contact without them trying to sell you something you don't want. Only offer your customers something they are likely to want. Do it no more than once a year with each customer.

As well as these direct requests, you should also be able to find ways to market your services more subtly. If you send monthly bills to your customers, why not include some information about another service they could take from you? Or if you provide sales receipts, how about attaching a money-off coupon for their next visit?

Or be even more subtle about it and simply use these communication avenues to provide your customers with good news about your company. However you approach it, don't ignore this potential source of new sales.

19 Use existing customers to get new customers

Personal recommendation is the most powerful marketing tool at your disposal. Think about when you last bought something. Whether it was a holiday, a car or just a film for rent, you were probably persuaded by the recommendations of others. Think also about the numbers involved. If you have 100 customers, and if just ten of them recommend you to ten people, that's 100 people who have received a personal and powerful reason to buy from you.

Your existing customers are an excellent source of these referrals, and very often growing businesses fail to tap into them. The worry is that once you've sold to them and then cross-sold them another product, if you start asking them to recommend you to others, they'll think you're just pestering them and you'll lose their custom.

This is rarely the case. You will almost certainly find it much easier than you think to persuade your existing customers to give you these recommendations. For one thing, if they've already bought from you the chances are that they think highly of your products or services. If you have some way of monitoring customer satisfaction you will know which ones are most likely to give you a positive recommendation. Few people would be offended by a polite request along those lines.

If you feel your customers need more of a push to recommend you, consider setting up an incentive scheme. You could offer 10 per cent off their next purchase for each lead they give you. Offer more if the referral will turn into long-term business for you. It almost always makes sense to charge less now to gain a new long-term source of income.

20 Approach a new market

It can be easy to become stuck in one market. Just because your clients have always been lawyers it doesn't mean you have to stick with that market. Would your products not be relevant to accountants, property management firms or any other professional service provider?

Even if your products are selling well in one market it is a good idea to diversify as insurance against problems in that market. Whatever you sell, think about who else could benefit from it. Could you open up new premises in a new town? What about selling overseas? Are there new sectors you could move into? Are you focusing on one age group, income group or gender, to the exclusion of others?

21 Sell something new

Just as it can be easy to become stuck in one market, so we can become so fixated on producing, marketing and selling our products or services we forget to innovate, to offer the market something new. Establish a culture of continual innovation. Talk to your customers to find out what they want and then give it to them. Encourage your staff to come up with ideas for innovation.

Hungry for ideas on how to take your marketing online at very little cost? You'll find many in the next chapter. First, here is the story of a company that used a powerful promotion strategy.

Case study
Episys

Derek Buchanan joined Episys as CEO five years ago, and since then he has developed a highly sophisticated and effective promotional programme which costs almost nothing and has doubled the company's turnover from £3.5 million to £7 million.

'If I went back home to Scotland, and told my mum how well I'm doing, she'd tell me off for being big-headed,' Buchanan says. 'However, if someone from her bowling club said the same thing to her she'd be immensely proud. This is the fundamental principle behind our marketing – rather than spend money on ads that tell everyone how great we are, we earn the right by successfully delivering their projects, so our clients say it for us.'

Founded in 1987, Cambridge-based Episys provides in-store signage and product labelling to companies such as B&Q, Comet, Fortnum & Mason, John Lewis Partnership, Marks & Spencer, Sainsbury's and Waitrose. Five years ago when Buchanan joined, it was doing fine, but he saw the need to focus on customer relationships and to grow through referrals rather than through costly marketing initiatives.

In every contract it has with its clients Episys includes the request that if Episys does what it promises, the client will provide references. Some of these are used in the media to generate positive editorial coverage. Others are used as case studies at the marketing events that the company runs. It holds one major European event every May, three a year in the USA and monthly executive briefings on both sides of the Atlantic.

Buchanan recalls that five years ago he struggled to get half a dozen people into a room above a café in north London. In May 2008 the company held its biggest-ever event, when it brought 500 clients, prospects and partners together for a one-day event at Wembley Stadium. The cost was kept low by involving technology partners who also wanted access to this audience of buyers, but much of the day was taken up by Episys clients describing how they have successfully worked with the company.

'It's by far the best form of marketing,' says Buchanan. 'Over lunch our customers share their experiences with prospective customers enabling those prospects to make positive decisions about becoming clients. In the three months right after that event we gained £500,000 worth of sales from people who had attended it. That figure will increase in time.'

Of course, not every company would be happy to let their existing customers talk to their sales prospects. The fact that every Episys employee knows this will happen serves to focus their attention very strongly on customer satisfaction. The company's clients are happy to have this clause written into the contracts, because it is the best guarantee of good service they could possibly get.

Buchanan concludes with this advice on running similar events:
'Send out invites at least 90 days in advance, and confirm by phone. This dramatically reduces cancellations. Be open with your customers. Provide them with the products and service they want. Then put on

informative and entertaining events to attend, where they can tell others about what a great job you've done for them. Do all that and you cannot fail to grow your business.'

Key points

→ Promoting your business need not be expensive or overly time consuming.

→ Set up a promotional ideas file and encourage everyone in your business to add to it.

→ Once a month start doing one of the 21 ideas in this chapter or one of the ideas in your ideas file.

Next steps

What action will you take to apply the information in this chapter? By when will you do it?

_____

_____

_____

_____

When I took office, only high energy physicists had ever heard of what is called the Worldwide Web. Now even my cat has its own page. Bill Clinton

DIY online marketing that boosts sales

This isn't 2001

This chapter isn't going to tell you about the potential of the internet for growing businesses. It's not going to give you all the usual waffle you see in business books about how the internet is the small business's shop window to the world. I'm assuming you know this already.

This chapter isn't even going to offer you advice on how to build a website that looks professional, is easy to use and is kept up to date. If you're not doing all that already, then get a shift on. This isn't 2001.

The game has moved on. Instead, I want to show you what web-savvy small businesses are doing online right now to increase their sales with minimal investment. I want to give you straightforward steps you can follow in order to replicate that success.

You don't need to hire expensive consultants or uncommunicative techies to do all this. You can do it yourself with a surprisingly small amount of money.

However, be warned – it is not free. One of the greatest mistakes the growing business makes is to believe that marketing online is free. They end up dabbling, looking amateurish and doing more long-term damage than good to their sales figures. Don't fall into this trap. Read through the following guides and approach these new techniques with due care and caution.

Do it properly and you'll be amazed at how well it works.

Affiliate marketing – risk-free advertising?

Imagine if you only had to pay for television ads once they resulted in actual sales. Imagine if you could see exactly who was watching your ads, where those viewers came from and what they did after seeing your ad. Imagine if the ads were shown to a worldwide audience of people, all of whom were watching that channel because they were actually shopping for what you sell.

It would be too good to be true, wouldn't it? Well, no actually. That is exactly what online affiliate marketing can offer you.

An **affiliate** is an online publisher, a website owner. Through affiliate marketing you agree that they will show your ads on their site, and when someone clicks through that ad and buys from you, you pay the affiliate either a fixed sum or, more commonly, a percentage of the money you make.

It began back in 1996 with Amazon's associates' programme, and was then restricted to books, CDs and DVDs. However, it has spread rapidly and is now used by almost all sectors. Its growth has accelerated in recent years as consumers have become more and more confident at buying almost everything online. Back in 2001 we may have bought a CD online, but now many of us will happily buy cars, holidays and even mortgages online.

Consider where you go to buy any of those products online. You may have a provider that you always trust, but it's more likely that you will consult a review site or a price comparison site. It's little surprise then that these sites, which we visit when we're considering making a purchase, have emerged as among the most popular affiliate marketing sites. They are not the only ones though. Others include specialist interest sites, popular blog sites and coupon-based reward sites.

More and more advertisers are realising the power of affiliate marketing and are getting in on the act, and the industry is growing at an exponential rate. Getting started as an advertiser is relatively straightforward. You simply approach one of the many affiliate networks and they will get your ad placed on suitable sites.

They will take some of your revenue for doing this, on top of the percentage that you will already have to pay the affiliate, so understandably some advertisers prefer to approach specific affiliates directly. There is nothing to stop you doing that. Search online for sites that your potential customers will visit, and offer that site a percentage of any revenue you receive from customers who reach you through an ad on its site. You will need to invest in some fairly simple code to enable you to track this online traffic, but most web developers should be able to produce this for you at little cost.

You need to liaise with your networks to give them online ads that appeal to their particular audience. You also need to keep them updated on special offers or events that will encourage their visitors to visit your site, and you need to build strong relationships with them.

The affiliates only get paid when you do, so the onus is on you to make the partnership work, especially when it comes to the more popular sites, where you'll be one of many advertisers competing for space. However, pick the right affiliates and work with them to build powerful campaigns and you could give your sales a huge boost with very little financial risk.

Producing marketing emails that people read

Email really ought to be the perfect marketing medium. Most people have email, your potential customers can go from your email to your website with the click of a button, it costs nothing to send, anyone can produce a marketing email, and you can track exactly how recipients respond to every email you send.

Yet, for many companies, email marketing has been a major letdown. You might have experienced this yourself. You might have tried buying a list of email addresses, emailed them with some information about your products, services or company, and then been disappointed by how few responded. If so, you're not alone – many businesses have been down this route, and most have given up on email marketing.

It's understandable, but it's a pity, because email marketing really can work. You just have to get it right. Don't do email marketing solely because it's cheap. It is cheap compared with many offline forms of marketing, but that doesn't mean it's free.

First of all, you need to invest in proper data. Just as with postal direct mail, firing off email after email to a poorly researched list of contacts usually does more harm than good. So, aim for a shorter list, and make it one that has accurate addresses, isn't getting caught up in a spam filter and is comprised of people who will be genuinely interested in what you're selling.

Don't be fooled into thinking that just because you don't get many bouncebacks and not many people are unsubscribing that you have a good list – recipients may just be deleting your emails as soon as they arrive. Don't even look to open rates for reassurance – recipients may just be opening them and deleting them straight away. Assessing the number of recipients in this second group, the so-called 'silent deleters', is almost impossible, but you should be able to reduce their numbers first by improving your data quality, and then by giving people content they value.

In other words

Bouncebacks are emails that are returned to you unread.

The email inbox is a busy place. There are many, many other people competing there for the attention of your potential customers. So you need to send them something that interests them. It's not enough just to tell them about your products or services. However exciting they are to you, they're probably much less so to your recipients.

What will work for your customers?

You're the best judge of what will excite your customers. It might be coupons for money off your products. It might be an insightful white paper on a current industry topic. It might be a competition to win an exciting prize. Or it might be news that they can't get elsewhere. Whatever it is, it needs to grab their attention rapidly and make them look forward to receiving more emails from you.

If you send someone something that isn't interesting to them three times then they almost certainly will unsubscribe from your list. If, though, you can capture their interest just once you have the beginnings of a relationship.

Build on that relationship by integrating your email marketing with other marketing, such as telemarketing, direct mail or the offers you promote on your website. Continue to provide recipients with something they value, and you will soon see the results come through.

Once you've worked on your data quality, content and integration, try the following to improve your email marketing campaigns:

1 Consistency – devise a central template so that recipients can easily recognise emails from your organisation.

2 Call to action – make it clear what you want people to do after reading your email, and make it very easy for them to do it.

3 Subject line – the initial decision to delete or read will be made on the subject line, so make sure it reflects the content of the email and grabs the reader's attention.

4 Personalisation – make every email as individual as possible, at least by using the recipient's name.

5 Subscriptions – you must always offer a clear, straightforward opt-out/unsubscribe option, but consider also offering recipients the chance to receive different content, to have more or less regular emails and so on.

How to improve your search engine ranking

What do you do when you want to buy something online? If you know of a review site or a price comparison site you probably go there. If you don't know of one the chances are that you'll use a search engine, probably Google. When the results come up you know that those in the right-hand column are paid for, so you'll probably click on those in the left-hand column, assuming that their high rankings mean they're high-quality companies.

A vast amount of sales are begun in this way. And that's why entrepreneurs like you are so keen on search engine optimisation (SEO). This is about getting your site to appear high on those search engine rankings. It is fast becoming one of the most popular forms of marketing, and when you consider your own recent online purchases it is easy to see why.

While SEO can be extremely effective, it is also extremely complicated. Search engines use complex algorithms to rank websites, and SEO is essentially about understanding how these algorithms work and how to maximise a site's chances of scoring highly on them. There are now thousands of experts who will help you do this, but you can make a good start on your own by following these five steps.

1 Know what's hot

The first step is to find out what terms people are searching for online. There are several online tools that will allow you to do this for free, most notably Google's Insight for Search. It allows you to track certain words and phrases, to see when and where people are searching for them. Through these tools you'll be able to work out which keywords you should be using on your site. You'll find them at **www.google.com/ insights/search**.

2 Give your website the right name

The most important words on your website are the domain name, so make sure your domain name both reflects what your business does and includes words that people are searching for frequently. Bear in mind, however, that for most search engine algorithms the age of a domain name is a positive factor, so it's always best to get your domain name right at the outset.

3 Use keywords, keywords, keywords

You can also alert the search engines to your website's relevance to a particular keyword by including that keyword in as many places as possible. Use it in file names and folders and in your page titles. Rather than getting visitors to click on images to navigate around your site, get them to click on keywords. Use these keywords in your text, but be careful not to overdo it. It's all well and good optimising your site so well that it attracts legions of visitors, but if all they find there is ungrammatical gibberish they'll soon leave.

4 Keep it fresh

The more often you update your content, the more frequently the search engines look at your site to see what is there. So build in time to make small, frequent changes to your site.

5 Get listed in a web directory

The search engines like sites that have incoming links. So, if you can have your site promoted on another site, you will boost your ranking. You may need to do two-way deals with other website owners to achieve this, or you can pay for a listing on DMOZ, a highly regarded web directory. You'll find it online at **www.dmoz.org**.

Web 2.0 – hype or business opportunity?

I'm sure you've heard of Web 2.0. It's the latest internet buzz-phrase, but unlike many internet buzz-phrases it does in fact describe something that you can use to grow your business.

While Web 1.0 was about you broadcasting to your customers, Web 2.0 is about you interacting with them. Today's successful websites are those that allow visitors to comment on content, add to that content and feel a part of the site.

There are several features you can add to your site to encourage and facilitate that interaction. Most of them are inexpensive and fairly straightforward to implement. Almost all though require a consistent investment of time over the long term, so you're better picking one feature and focusing on that rather than trying to do everything at once.

In the same way you should avoid overcomplicating your website with too many features – it's better to have one feature done brilliantly than a half-hearted attempt at several.

Blogs

The term 'blog' is a contraction of web log and is essentially an online series of postings by an individual or organisation. It is a way for you to share your thoughts, observations and expertise with potential customers. Crucially it also allows them to comment on your blogs, so it can act as the catalyst to a dialogue. Most blogs are little more than personal diaries, but a growing number of businesses are realising their potential as marketing tools.

Setting one up is very easy. You can do this on a range of sites, such as Wordpress, Typepad and Blogger, for only a small fee, or free if you're willing to accept other people's ads on your blog. You then need to choose the subject on which you'll blog. It needs to be about an aspect of your industry or your local area that matters to your readers, but more than anything you have to care about the subject. You'll need to come up with something interesting to say around once a day, so pick a topic on which you've got plenty to say.

Then you start writing. Aim to post at least five times a week. Make your posts short, insightful and entertaining. Check your spelling, grammar and factual accuracy. Encourage your existing customers to subscribe to it and leave comments. Read other blogs in your industry and leave comments there. Be patient and do not expect a worldwide following overnight. For an example, see the blog on our website, **www.forentrepreneursbooks.com**. It's a joint effort by the authors of the *For Entrepreneurs* series of books, with each author posting once a week.

There are more than 100 million blogs in the world, so you're competing in a crowded market. However, many of those blogs are redundant as the blogger has given up. Furthermore, few are run by people who have as much to say as you, or who are saying it in such an interesting way. So give it time, spend 15 minutes a day on it, every day, and before long you may find you have built a loyal following of readers and are picking up work as a result.

Toolkit

These are three sites that will help you get blogging quickly and cheaply:
www.typepad.com
www.blogger.co.uk
www.wordpress.org

Video and audio streaming

In the early Web 1.0 days online video got a bad reputation, as it usually involved cumbersome Flash plug-ins that made a site slow to download with the limited bandwidth most users had. However, those problems have by and large been overcome by new technology, and many growing businesses are finding that even using homemade material at very little cost they can significantly enhance the visitor experience on their websites.

You could show your product in action or your company at work, or simply film yourself talking about the benefits of your product. Even better, ask one of your customers to do it. Show visitors something interesting and they are much more likely to stay on your site and come back. Remember to introduce fresh content or it will soon look out of date.

Viral games and videos

Just as in the real world, the best form of marketing is word of mouth, so you should do all you can to encourage visitors to your website to tell their friends and colleagues about it. One way of doing this is creating content that they want to share with others.

We've all seen those games and videos that do the rounds. Have you ever considered how rapidly they spread? The right content can reach millions of people right across the world in the space of a day. That's why this is called viral marketing.

You should be able to hire a freelancer to do the necessary programming for little outlay. The greatest challenge is coming up with something that's fun and catchy but that also promotes your products. Be careful with viral marketing – get it wrong and you could do irreparable damage to your reputation. But get it right and you could get your product in front of more people than you ever thought possible.

User-generated content

Perhaps the best way of getting your visitors engaged in your website is to give them the opportunity to create the content. A large part of the attraction of Amazon is the ability to write reviews of films, albums and books and to read others' reviews before making purchases. This sort of interaction gives visitors a sense of ownership and makes them want to come back time after time to view or post new content.

Think about how you could allow your visitors to post content on your site. Could they discuss how best to use your product? Could they vote on an industry issue? Could they post reviews, pictures or videos?

Toolkit

You can use content-sharing sites such as Flickr and YouTube to host the content and then link it to your site, making this a very affordable, and potentially very effective, add-on. You'll find them at:

www.flickr.com for photos;

www.youtube.com for videos.

Seven things you can do online right now for free to grow your business

1 Change your email signature so it does more than just provide your name, company and phone number – what more could you tell people about there?

2 Set up an online poll. You can add one of these to your website very easily and very cheaply. People like to vote, and think what you could do with the results.

3 Post on a discussion board. One of the best ways to encourage people to engage with your site is to engage with theirs.

4 Put your URL on your offline marketing. Is it absolutely everywhere it could be?

5 Set up a system to ensure you respond to online requests within 24 hours – *every* time.

6 Visit your website and look at it through the eyes of a first-time visitor – or even better, find someone to do this mystery shopping for you. Is it really as user-friendly as you think? Does it really convey the messages you want it to?

7 Ask subscribers to your email newsletter to tell their friends and colleagues about it.

The other crucial skill that you need is sales, and you'll find the entire next chapter dedicated to how you can acquire it. First, here is a case study of a company that used internet marketing to rocket to success.

Case study
Webcredible

When he founded Webcredible in February 2004, Trenton Moss didn't even have space in his spare room for an office, so he worked in the hallway, using only a PC, internet connection and phone. Now the web usability and accessibility consultancy employs 18 people and turns over £1.5 million a year.

How to Grow your Business for Entrepreneurs

It works for organisations such as the BBC, EDF Energy, the Ministry of Defence, Norwich Union, Sony, T-Mobile, Thomson and the World Health Organisation, helping them make their websites easier for visitors to use. Moss attributes almost all of this growth to his online marketing work.

Webcredible's website features all the usual company information you might expect, but also offers more than 150 free articles and white papers. Moss says: 'We've invested a lot of time writing these educational, how-to articles over the years, always ensuring that we write in a chatty, informative and informal style.'

'Our competitors have always been very guarded with their knowledge,' he explains. 'They've only been willing to share even the basics once hired by a client. We've taken the opposite approach and have actively shared our expertise in these high quality articles on our website. The result has been that we're now widely recognised as industry-leading knowledge experts.'

'In deciding which articles to write, the team uses free keyword tools such as Google AdWords Keyword Tool to find what topics people are searching for. Consequently the articles draw fresh visitors to the website. It receives 8,000 visitors every day, a remarkable number for a B2B company of its size. In fact Webcredible's site traffic is greater than the sum of its ten main competitors'.

Two-thirds of that traffic comes from Google, on which the agency is usually in the top three for its 20 or so service offerings. It has achieved this high ranking by optimising each of its pages around a specific phrase and generating in-bound links to its website. Moss explains: 'Every time another website links to the Webcredible website Google sees this link and counts it as a "vote" for our website. The more votes a website has, all other things being equal, the higher up in the rankings the website appears.'

These in-bound links have therefore been important. Webcredible has achieved them by actively encouraging other websites to republish its articles for free, provided they give an author biography with links back to the Webcredible site.

The agency does a limited amount of advertising online, mostly through Google AdWords, the adverts that appear in search results on the right side of the page. Moss says: 'This form of advertising is very effective as you only pay when someone clicks on your advert. The amount you pay per click depends on how much you're willing to bid. The more you bid, the higher in the listings your advert appears and the more likely your advert is to get clicked. By choosing niche phrases ahead of more general phrases, we were able to appear higher in the listings whilst bidding smaller amounts.'

When it launched its website the company also launched a monthly newsletter. Just 26 people signed up to receive the first newsletter, but there are now more than 18,000 subscribers. Moss says: 'The reason for its popularity is that we don't try to sell our services in the newsletter. Rather, we share knowledge and provide our subscribers with useful information on ways to practically improve their websites.'

Moss is not about to rest on his laurels. He has recently set up RSS feeds, where people can republish links to his articles, along with short article descriptions, directly on their website. This means that every time Webcredible publishes a new article this list automatically updates on the other organisation's website.

It is also about to embark on a social media campaign. It will be encouraging users of social bookmarking sites such as Digg and del.icio.us to link back to specific articles on the Webcredible site. The more people that link to an article, the higher in the site hierarchy the link is and the more likely it is that people will follow that link.

Moss offers this advice on how to optimise your site: 'SEO is a relatively straightforward activity. You need to identify which keyword phrases people are using. You can do this with a tool such as Google AdWords. Then you need to create pages optimised around one phrase by placing that phrase in the page title, headings and in links pointing at that page. Finally you need to have other websites link to your site.'

He concludes:

'While it's straightforward it is also phenomenally time-consuming so don't underestimate that aspect. It is though without doubt time well spent.'

Web bonus

At our website, **www.forentrepreneursbooks.com**, click on the 'How to Grow Your Business' button. On the link for Chapter Nine you'll read advice from a search engine optimisation expert on how to get your site to the top of the rankings.

How to Grow your Business for Entrepreneurs

Key points

→ Having a basic website is no longer enough if you want to take advantage of the potential of the internet for growing your business.

→ Get started in affiliate marketing.

→ Produce marketing emails that people read.

→ Improve your search engine rankings.

→ Use blogs, online videos and viral marketing to build an online community.

Next steps

What action will you take to apply the information in this chapter? By when will you do it?

_____

_____

_____

_____

Everyone lives by selling something.

Robert Louis Stevenson

Mastering the art of sales

Chapter Ten

Business is sales

Whatever type of business you're in you need to know how to sell. Of all the topics covered in this book, it's probably the most important. If you can't sell you're going to struggle.

The type of selling you do depends very much on the type of business you run. If it's a business-to-business company with a handful of large corporate clients, you will need to be able to get appointments with new prospects and convert those initial meetings into clients. Your business will be utterly dependent on your sales skills.

If it's a consumer-facing retail business then once you have the customer in your shop, bar, restaurant or whatever, much of the work is done. So, the marketing and promotional activities we've already covered will probably be more important to you. However, you will still have to be able to use sales skills to relate to that customer and provide good customer service.

You will also require sales skills in other aspects of your work. You may need to sell your business plan to your bank manager or investors. You may need to sell your expansion ideas to a planning committee. Or one day you may need to sell your business.

There's no escaping it – entrepreneurs have to be able to sell, and the better you are at selling the more successful your enterprise will be.

Telesales is not a dirty word

Many entrepreneurs shy away from the telephone as a sales tool. Given the reputation that telephone sales has this is hardly surprising. We've all experienced the awkward sales call from people who are obviously reading from a script, and who seem to be racing to get as many words in before we interrupt or hang up.

Anyone who has put aside these reservations and tried selling over the phone knows how difficult it can be. Few people have the time to talk, and it's very difficult to tell them how much they could gain from your product or service. A few hours of demoralising rejections is usually enough to put most people off.

They'll either forget all about using the telephone as a sales tool or will foist the job on to a junior member of staff. All too often this involves sitting that hapless employee down with a directory, a telephone and some vague advice about smiling and dialling. Unsurprisingly this rarely does much to fill the order book. It usually does more to open up a junior vacancy at the company in question.

It doesn't have to be like this. Done well, telemarketing is a cost-effective, measurable and scalable activity. Regardless of the type of business you run, you should consider how it could help grow your business. Who could you sell to over the phone? Who could you get an appointment with that could lead to new business?

Ten steps to sales success

Some people believe that they were not born to sell, that they are more suited to technical or creative work. While it is true that some people are born salespeople, it is equally true that you can learn to be a good salesperson. It is like any skill – if you have enough motivation, if you get the right training and if you practise enough, you will succeed at it.

Whether you are a sales novice or veteran, the following ten steps will give you some pointers on how you can improve your sales technique and grow your business.

Preparation

Whether you are doing the selling yourself or you are delegating it to one of your team, you need to begin armed with all the details about the product or service you are selling. If it is over the phone then avoid the temptation to use scripts. Think about your own reaction when you're called by salespeople using scripts. Your prospects will be able to tell whether someone is reading from a script and will immediately switch off.

Instead you need to develop a briefing sheet, detailing the features and benefits of what you're selling, describing a short, simple introduction and outlining some intelligent questions you can ask. It should also cover all the practical information you will need, such as your phone number, email address and website address.

Face-to-face selling is a performance and, like an actor on a stage, you need to look the part. You need to have all your props and you need to rehearse until you can play your part almost without thinking. Ensure you know what you will wear, assemble your presenting materials and run through your presentation again and again until you know it inside out.

Danger!

Make sure you know where your meeting is and plan to arrive well in advance. There is nothing more likely to put you off than arriving late, flustered, to see a room full of people glancing angrily at their watches.

Know your prospects

As well as having a clear idea of what you are going to say, you need to know who you are going to target. The more tightly targeted your data, the fewer rejections you will have. You might want to revisit the sections in Chapter Seven on working out who your best prospects are and finding more like them. You may already have a list of prospects, or you may need to spend some time researching leads or use something like a delegate list from an event you attended. Or you may need to buy in some data.

Wherever you get your data, check it against the Corporate Telephone Preference Service or the consumer Telephone Preference Service to ensure there is no one on the list who has asked to be removed from telemarketers' lists. Also, if you are targeting businesses, bear in mind that people change jobs frequently, so even a list that is only one year old will contain a lot of redundant data.

In sales meetings, while you will need to prepare a standard sales pitch, you should always aim to tailor it to each specific audience. To do this, and to appear credible during your meeting, you should thoroughly research your prospects beforehand. Find out about the individuals you're meeting, the company, the sector. Think about the issues they are facing and adapt your presentation accordingly.

Getting past the gatekeepers

This stage is specifically relevant to telephone sales and is in fact one of the most difficult elements, especially when you are approaching senior corporate buyers. Around nine out of ten calls you make will be blocked by receptionists and secretaries or will end up with a voicemail.

You can improve this ratio by sounding confident, as if you expect to be put through, and by finding out the times when your prospect tends to be in the office. Very often early morning or after hours is the best time to catch them as they're uninterrupted by other demands and their gatekeepers have either not arrived yet or gone home.

Mr Finster employed a particularly effective gatekeeper strategy.

The introduction

Once you have got hold of a decision maker on a sales call, be it a homeowner or a business buyer, you have around seven seconds to interest them. Unless you can capture their interest within that very short space of time, they will be thinking of ways to end the conversation. The same is true of face-to-face sales. You generally have longer, but not by much. You have no more than a few minutes to get your audience actively interested in your pitch or they'll switch off and start wondering about their next meeting or how soon they can get you out of their home or office.

The single biggest mistake that people make when they are selling is thinking that the way to interest a prospect is to talk at them. They believe that if they fill those crucial first minutes with as much information as possible, some of it will interest the audience and they'll be prepared to carry on listening.

Think of conversations you enjoy when you're at home, at a weekend talking to family members or friends, on the phone or in person. Do you enjoy those conversations where you're listening to someone telling you something? Or do you enjoy those where you get to do some of the talking?

The same is true of sales conversations. To make someone interested in your conversation you need to get them talking. You do that by asking them questions that they want to answer, questions that make them think. As a rule of thumb, in a successful sales conversation you should be talking roughly only 25 per cent of the time.

However, you do need to let the prospect know who you are. So prepare a concise, engaging opening statement. On the phone this need be no more than who you are, where you're calling from and why you're calling. In a sales meeting you may want to give a little more detail, but don't overdo it. Talk just enough to set the scene and then get the prospects involved.

Practise your introduction over and over again, so you sound calm, composed and confident.

Questions and building a dialogue

After your introduction you need to ask a question. It should be an open question – one that cannot be answered with a blunt 'yes' or 'no' – and it should interest the prospect. It needs to be relevant to that individual or the group. Think about what issues they might be facing in their job or life that your product or service can help with and frame your questions around that.

If you can get them talking, listen carefully and demonstrate that you've listened. Repeat their answer back to them, using different phrasing, and ask further questions based on their responses. This is the most difficult part and is where scripts fall down. It should be a natural dialogue, in which you're persuading the prospect to outline their need, and you're then explaining how you can meet that need.

It is difficult to do and requires patient practice. Over time you will develop a feel for what works and what doesn't. The key is not to be discouraged by early failure.

Very often with telephone sales it makes sense to start working on a section of your database that has the least desirable leads. Practise on those and hone your introduction, questions and selling points, so that you're fully prepared for tackling the best parts of your database.

Equally, the worst presentations are those where the presenter begins to talk about themselves or about their product or company, and then drones on for ages, providing irrelevant details. Very often people who give these presentations wonder why people don't seem to listen to them and try to enliven their talks by introducing some humour or technology. This misses the point. Your audience doesn't want jokes or flashy PowerPoint graphics. They want a solution to the challenges they face.

You should never begin to tell people what they need until you have clarified exactly what it is that they need. You may have discovered much of this in your phone call to arrange the meeting. If so, begin by going through what was covered on the phone, making sure that the situation is the same and that you have properly understood the need. If not, start from the beginning to ascertain the need.

Overcoming objections

Sometimes it works like a dream. Your introduction sets the scene and your initial question prompts an in-depth response. You then construct a dialogue that opens up a clear need for what you're selling and you convincingly explain how you can help meet that need.

But then it goes wrong. The prospect says they can't afford it, they haven't got time right now or they need to speak to someone else before they can make a decision. In even the best sales call or meeting you will almost certainly come up against objections like this.

Always acknowledge the objection. There is nothing more annoying than salespeople who persistently ignore your objections and just plough on with their sales spiel.

You will soon learn the main objections that you face. Time, budget and authority are very common ones, but you will encounter your own specific objections, depending on what you are selling to whom. The key is to prepare for them. Before your call or meeting, think about what you are likely to face and know how you will overcome it.

While you shouldn't back down at the first objection, equally you must be ready to accept that some objections are valid. If the prospect genuinely doesn't have the budget for your software then you're wasting your time. If they've just bought a new kitchen then you're wasting you're time. Just accept it, thank them for their attention and agree a good time for you to contact them again in the future.

And yet in some situations you should not give up so easily. Whether or not an objection is indeed valid will depend on exactly what you are selling and to whom. If they don't have the budget for your software, but you've identified a need for it, perhaps you could aim higher in the organisation at the person who allocates budgets. If they've just bought a new kitchen, do you have some ancillary products or services that you could sell them? Maybe they need some floor or wall tiles?

Closing

The good news is that once you've followed all the steps outlined so far, closing is easy. The close is in fact an overrated element of the sales call. Many salespeople put too much emphasis on it and so fail to do the groundwork. Once you've identified a need for your product or service, have convinced the prospect that your product or service can indeed meet that need and have overcome all objections, it should be a logical next step in the conversation to suggest they send you a cheque, you put a date in the diary for a meeting or whatever your close involves.

Negotiation

Few sales are simple 'yes' or 'no' affairs. Most involve some element of negotiation. Too many entrepreneurs take offence when someone offers them a lower price for their products or services. Don't become so emotionally involved in it. If someone's opening a negotiation with you they're not insulting you or your company – they're telling you they want to buy from you.

Preparation is essential to successful negotiation. Before your sales call or meeting, decide your negotiating parameters. What is the lowest price you can accept? What can you offer the prospect that they will value but will cost you little?

Too many people view negotiation as the art of getting as much as they can out of the other person. Those tend to be the businesses with very high customer turnover. If you want to enjoy repeat business or to encourage a recommendation, work so that both parties leave the negotiation feeling that they've got a good deal.

Agreeing next steps

Regardless of the outcome of the call or the meeting, you need to agree a next action with the prospect. That might be delivering the product, calling again in six months or removing them from your database. Whatever it is, there must be a concrete outcome and you, the salesperson, must own it.

A shocking number of potential sales fall through because the salesperson loses control of the process. Don't agree that the prospect will call you in a fortnight. They won't. Something else will distract them, because at the end of the day you have more interest in the sale going through than they do. Always make sure that you agree to do something that will move the relationship forward to its next logical stage.

Sticking at it

Finally, don't give up. Sales, especially telephone-based sales, can be incredibly demoralising, and it can take a long time to see results. It is easy to let the constant rejections put you off, and for you to spend your time on easier tasks instead. However, if you follow all the steps above and you keep at it for a long time, tracking prospects through a sales cycle, it will all pay off.

In Part Four you'll discover how to handle two elements of entrepreneurship that can trap the unwary entrepreneur, namely finance and legal issues. First, we end this chapter with a look at two companies that base much of their success on their innovative approaches to sales.

Case study
Fresh

Nick Porter has grown his creative communications company from launch to a business turning over £6.25 million in just four years. He has done this by picking up contracts from the likes of Marks & Spencer, Abbey, NPower and Comet. Fresh manages events such as product launches and sales conferences, and for many of these jobs Porter has been competing against the likes of Jack Morton, a world famous firm that has organised Olympic opening ceremonies. Porter wins around 60 per cent of all pitches he attends. Clearly he knows a thing or two about sales.

He says: 'The first thing to get right is make sure you're selling to the right person. Invest in a good database software product like ACT! And keep it up to date. If someone is no longer relevant remove them from the database. Don't waste time continuing to contact them. Also before you phone someone up you should send them an email to qualify that they're the right person. If they are then when you call they know who you are, and if they're not they'll usually refer you to the right person and then you've got an introduction.'

He concludes:

'The key to our success is that we don't just take briefs from our clients. We ask them why they want to hold this event, and we listen to what they have to say. More than anything else, sales is about listening. Too many people come in and try to sell to me by just talking at me, not listening to what I want. We've got 300 potential clients on our database and if we can convert just one per cent of them into clients in the next two years we'll reach our target of a £10 million turnover. I'm confident that we'll be able to do it.'

How to Grow Your Business for Entrepreneurs

Case study
Totalamber

In 2004 Alan O'Neill was frustrated that his software consultancy Totalamber seemed to have become stuck on a turnover of between £2 million and £3 million. The company provides consultants to help businesses implement large software applications, and O'Neill felt that it had so much further to go.

'I'd launched back in 1997 after several years learning about the IT contractor recruitment market at Alexander Mann,' he recalls. 'I'd wanted to set up a different type of company in this market, one where the stakeholders during a sales process worked constructively together, rather than seeing each other as some kind of necessary evil.'

He continues: 'We'd grown well in the early years, partly because in the run up to Y2K software consultants were highly in demand. In the early years of this decade it started to get a lot harder. I was working non-stop, but still struggling to get my consultants placed. So, in 2004 I decided I needed to change something. I locked myself in a room and worked out what we had to offer that was different and how we needed to go about selling it.'

Since he emerged from that room O'Neill has put 50 per cent on Totalamber's turnover every year, and now owns a business that turns over £7 million a year on a 30 per cent profit margin. What he discovered in that room should therefore be of very great interest to any entrepreneur who wants to grow their company.

The most tangible output was a 75-step process for selling. It covers every stage in great detail, from preparation, through exploration, qualification, negotiation, closing and account development. He comments: 'It's all stuff that I've always done naturally, but the problem was that I wasn't sharing it with my team. So, I got it all down on paper and now I'm able to instil this process into every one of my 12 salespeople.'

O'Neill believes that there are certain aspects of sales that people are born with. For example, he is a firm believer in the importance of sensory acuity, the ability to pick up on the non-verbal indications of how others are responding to you. However, he believes that successful selling requires more than these innate abilities. It also requires training and practice.

Running through his approach to sales are two themes. First, he stresses the need to focus on what the prospect wants and needs rather than what you have to offer. He says: 'In the early years we only talked about the skills and experience of contractors who we had on our books, but our prospects weren't interested in this.'

He continues: 'It was only when we started engaging with prospects as people and showed how we were truly interested in the problems they were facing that we started to demonstrate precisely how our contractors could help them solve their problems. It was a turning point for our business.'

Second, he believes that the most important element in sales is control. He explains: 'The salesperson has to stay in control of the process at every stage. Never leave it up to the prospect to contact you. That's when relationships drift and sales fall through. It's up to you as the salesperson to own the process from start to finish.'

Totalamber has just taken on two new sales staff, and O'Neill is confidently looking forward to growing his business to £12 million turnover in 2009.

He concludes:

'By really focusing on our sales strategy and process we've transformed the business, and proved that we have a long, long way to go yet.'

Key points

→ Successful selling is a vital skill for anyone who wants to grow their business.

→ Don't be afraid to use the telephone as a sales tool.

→ Prepare fully.

→ Be concise in your sales pitch and do all you can to get your prospect talking.

→ Remember that negotiation is about reaching a mutually acceptable deal, not about getting as much as you can out of the other person.

→ Don't be deterred by early failures – successful selling takes a lot of practice but is worthwhile when you succeed.

Next steps

What action will you take to apply the information in this chapter? By when will you do it?

_____

_____

_____

_____

Growing your finances and staying legal

Part Four

He who does not economise
will have to agonise.   Confucius

Cut your outgoings

Chapter Eleven

Profit not thrift

There are two ways to increase your profits: sell more or spend less. While ideally you will do both, it should be noted before we go any further with this chapter that cost-cutting is very rarely the way to grow a company. Indeed, it can often produce the opposite result.

As we have seen throughout this book, growth requires investment. Investment in yourself, in your staff and in sales and marketing. Cutting back in any of those areas is likely to reduce the growth of your company.

This is not to say that you can't spend your money more wisely in those areas, and hopefully the preceding advice will help you to do that. But you should always be wary of cutting back in either staff development or marketing. Both are vital to the growth of your company.

However, by cutting back unnecessary expenditure in other areas, you can boost your profits, as well as generate more capital to invest in the parts of your business that will promote growth.

I'm sure you can think of many costs that you'd like to cut back. In recent years every business and consumer in the UK has suffered with soaring energy and fuel bills. Then there are the rapidly rising costs of raw materials and, of course, the ever-present tax burden.

> ## The engine that drives enterprise is not thrift, but profit. JOHN MAYNARD KEYNES

Five tips for legally cutting your tax bill

Tax evasion is of course illegal, and you should always seek your accountant's advice before taking any steps to try to reduce your tax bill. However, you should never leave your tax affairs entirely up to your accountant. Not only do you have a much greater incentive to reduce your tax bill than even the most conscientious of accountants does, but you only have your own business to worry about, while your accountant probably has many clients to keep happy.

Larger companies can afford to hire teams of in-house finance officers, and as a result they legally cut their tax bills by millions and millions of pounds every year. By knowing all of your rights and options you too can cut your tax bill. At the very least there are five topics you can ask your accountant about to ensure they're doing everything they should be.

Research and development

In an attempt to encourage innovation, the Government has introduced generous allowances for investment in research and development, and you ought to ensure you take advantage of them. You can deduct up to 150 per cent of qualifying expenditure over £10,000 when calculating profit for tax purposes. Furthermore, you can claim on revenues dated back to April 2000.

Toolkit

For further information on allowances, see the website of HM Revenue & Customs: **http://www.hmrc.gov.uk/randd/**.

Business equipment

Know the rates for which you are allowed to offset purchases of business equipment, such as furniture, IT equipment, tools, machines and so on. The main capital allowance is 20 per cent, but most small companies can claim a 40 per cent allowance in the first year of trading. In some cases, you can claim 100 per cent in the year following purchase. The rates change year by year, so check with your accountant or local tax office – but make sure you're claiming as much as you can.

Toolkit

Business Link's website contains a great deal of useful information on managing your company's tax affairs. It includes an interactive tool for working out your allowances on capital expenditure. You'll find it at **http://www.businesslink.gov.uk**.

Bank interest

You can offset all finance charges against tax. That includes payments on overdrafts and loans, as well as bank charges, credit card charges and payments on alternative finance arrangements, such as hire purchase and leasing.

Pensions

The Government is desperate to encourage pension savings, and so it allows tax relief on employer contributions to registered pension schemes. They are consequently an outstandingly tax-efficient way of rewarding employees, and no entrepreneur should ignore them.

Toolkit

The website of the Government's Pension Service contains a detailed employer's guide to company pension schemes. It's at **www.thepensionservice.gov.uk**.

The right year-end date

As an employer you hold on to substantial tax revenue, and the longer you hold on to it the better your cash flow will be and the more interest you can accrue. So, if possible, aim to set your year end for just before you generate the greatest part of your revenue.

For example, many retailers make around a third of their sales at Christmas, so by setting its year end for mid-November a £1 million turnover retailer could hold on to around £100,000 of tax revenue for a year and make several thousand pounds in interest.

Slash your fuel and energy bills

Between 2004 and 2006 business customers saw price increases in the region of 75 per cent for electricity and over 200 per cent for gas. During 2007 and 2008 the trend continued upwards, with the price of crude oil hitting ever new heights. In the same way, a litre of petrol which cost 54p in 1991 had by mid-2008 soared to over £1.20.

As a result, every business in the country has seen its fuel bills growing month by month in the past few years. As fossil fuel stocks decline, and the technology to provide alternative energy sources remains ever elusive, we are not likely to see those bills shrink in the near future. In fact they will become an ever greater problem for small businesses. While large companies can absorb these increases, for entrepreneurs they are becoming a significant expense and a major concern.

There is much that you can do. By picking the right supplier and doing everything you can to reduce your energy usage and fuel consumption, you can slash hundreds, even thousands, of pounds from these bills. You can take comfort in the fact that by doing so, you are not only improving your profit margins, but you are also helping to protect the environment for future generations.

Work out how much fuel you are currently using

Bills for gas and electricity tend to be confusing. Some cynics claim that energy companies do this deliberately to stop us realising how much we are paying for our gas and electricity. Whatever the reason, you need to work out exactly what is being spent where and when. If necessary, call your supplier and ask for a detailed breakdown of usage. In the same way, you should find out which of your employees are spending company money on fuel, why they are doing it, when and where.

Reduce energy consumption in the office

Once you have worked out where all this energy is being used, you will immediately be able to spot ways to be more efficient. Do you need to leave lights and heating on overnight? Are you leaving computers and other electronic equipment on standby overnight? How often are windows left open when the heating is on full power?

Laptop, mobile phone and PDA chargers continue to charge, using up to 95 per cent of the power, even when no longer attached to the device. So unplug all these chargers overnight.

The ideal temperature for an office is 19°C. If you lower your temperature settings by just one degree centigrade, you will reduce your heating bill by around 8 per cent a year.

Reduce the amount you pay per unit for your energy

If you still use your regional supplier you can almost certainly reduce your gas and electricity bills. There are several online price comparison websites that can show you which supplier will give you the best price. You should know when your contract is due for renewal, and start looking for an alternative provider six weeks before then. Look at longer-term two- or three-year fixed price contracts. These allow you to know how much you will be paying, and sometimes the longer the term the better the price you can get.

How to Grow Your Business for Entrepreneurs

Go to fewer business meetings

Fast broadband connections and innovative software mean that there are now many viable alternatives to the traditional business meeting. The best online conferencing software allows you to see participants onscreen, to talk and message each other in real-time and even to work on documents together.

For certain types of meeting these online conferences can be even more useful than an actual face-to-face meeting. Human interaction is of course essential for some meetings, but you could really slash your travel budget by investing in these new systems.

Time saver

Are all of your business meetings essential? Go through your diary now. Which of your meetings could be dealt with better by email or telephone? Encourage your employees to do the same with their diaries.

Cut fuel expenditure

When you or your employees absolutely do have to travel, there is much you can do to limit fuel wastage. Journey sharing can cut the fuel costs of a meeting by two, three or even four times. Fuel prices across the UK, or even across the same town or city, can vary by up to 10 per cent, so find out where the cheapest fuel is and ensure that all your employees buy fleet fuel there.

Then consider how well your employees are driving. Revving the engine unnecessarily and accelerating too quickly can use around 20 per cent more fuel than driving more conservatively. Issue all staff with a fuel card so you can monitor which ones are using the most fuel per mile travelled. Finally, consider investing in more fuel-efficient vehicles.

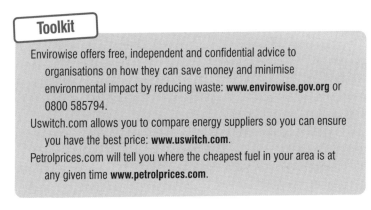

How to buy better

As you grow, you will find that you need to bring in more and more
external consultants and agents to help with various parts of your business. In fact, you may even find that getting this sort of help becomes
essential to your growth.

Just as many entrepreneurs struggle to delegate, many find it hard
to deal with consultants and agents. They tend to have the same reservations about entrusting their business to someone else, someone who
hasn't gone through all the hard work of setting it up and getting it to
this stage.

I have seen far too many examples of where these relationships
have gone wrong. Sometimes it's been the supplier's fault. But more
often than not it's been the entrepreneur's fault. They've not had a clear
reason for outsourcing, they've picked the wrong supplier, they've
agreed a poor deal or they've managed the relationship badly.

It ends up costing money and damaging the business. Perhaps this
has happened to you. Or perhaps you've seen it happen to other entrepreneurs and so now steer well clear of all suppliers, apart from the
entirely essential ones.

It is a mistake to ignore the value that suppliers can bring to your
enterprise. Whether it is finance, human resources, the law, marketing,
organisational development, strategy, quality management, technology
or facilities management, there is an ocean of talent out there, and by
approaching it correctly you can land yourself a skilled and experienced expert for a relatively low cost.

Here are five steps you can follow to ensure you procure successfully every time.

Work out why you want external help

A remarkable number of these relationships go wrong even before they've started, because the buyer decides a product or a service is needed before working out the precise problem that it will solve or the benefit it will bring. For example, it's decided a designer is needed to put together a new website, rather than working out what value that designer will bring, or even why a new website is wanted.

Begin with a clear understanding of what this supplier is going to add to your business. If it's a product, what will it enable you to do that you couldn't do before? Can you adapt what you already have to do the job equally well? If it's a service, what skills, knowledge or resources will they bring? Why do you need those skills, knowledge or resources? Is there no one that can do it in-house? Would it be more cost effective to hire or train someone to do it full-time?

When comparing the costs of external consultants and in-house staff, it can be tempting to baulk at the rates consultants charge. However, if you only need a £500-a-day consultant for 30 days a year, they're cheaper than a full-time employee on £15,000 a year once you've paid National Insurance and all the other costs associated with full-time employees. Furthermore, if they're charging £500 a day they should be much more experienced and capable than anyone you'd hire for £15,000.

Know what you're looking for

Once you know precisely why you want to spend your hard-earned money on an external supplier, you need to decide exactly what you're looking for. Many entrepreneurs find they can prioritise their requirements by writing down what the supplier must have, what it should have and what they would like it to have. Is it essential that it's local to you, or is relevant experience working for businesses like yours more important to you?

Think carefully about all the factors until you're clear in your own mind exactly what you need from the supplier. There are few golden rules in this area, as your requirements are unique to you, but I would strongly urge you to consider these three points before hiring any external supplier:

1 Steer well clear of anyone who babbles jargon or management-speak at you. It's always possible that they might be geniuses who are too clever to communicate with ordinary people, but it's much, much more likely that they don't know what they're talking about and are trying to cover this up by confusing you. Ask them to explain themselves more clearly. If they can't do it, strike them off your list.

2 Don't work with companies who are doing it for nothing, even if the company is owned by your best friend. Your work will be bottom of their list of priorities and the people working on it will resent it.

3 If you are hiring a consultant who you will work closely with over a period of time, make sure you can get on with them. Factual criteria such as relevant qualifications, skills and experience are of course important, but if you just don't get on with someone the relationship is very unlikely to work out.

Run a rigorous selection process

Begin with desk research. Try to find out who are the best suppliers in this area: search the internet, look at magazines, ask trade associations, visit conferences and check out what your competitors are doing – who do they use?

Once you have a list of potential suppliers contact them to ask if they would like to be considered for the contract. Invite those who are interested in for an exploratory meeting. Outline to them what you want to achieve. Get to know them and check you can work with them.

If possible, make an informal visit to the supplier's premises. You can find out much more than you might expect from things like the décor, the expressions on people's faces as you walk around and the conversations you overhear whilst waiting in reception.

Even if you're entirely convinced that the supplier is ideal for you, always take up references. Call the referees and try to get as much detail as you can. If you're spending a lot on this contract look beyond the references. Look at the rest of their client list – do you know anyone who works at any of those companies who could give you an informal opinion?

Agree a deal that works for both parties

External suppliers are rarely cheap, and the better they are the more expensive they tend to be. In most cases you shouldn't accept their first price, but don't drive too hard a bargain. Many suppliers will accept a much lower price, but will simply make a corresponding reduction in the amount of time they spend working for you.

Ensure you agree a deal that they're as happy with as you are. If you've followed all the steps above you'll have picked the right one, and the end result will more than justify the expenditure.

There are a few things to consider when agreeing a price with a supplier. First of all, make sure you know what you're buying. Ask the supplier to detail exactly what you will receive for the price you agree and ensure there are no unexpected extras such as travel expenses, set-up charges and so on.

Second, think about how bulk buying can reduce your costs. Obviously this applies to purchases of products such as stationery, but you may also be able to negotiate discounts on services. For example, rather than calling in IT support and paying a one-off fee whenever you have a problem, would it be cheaper to set up an ongoing contract?

Finally, make sure you give the supplier a comprehensive and accurate brief at the start of the relationship. This can go a long way towards preventing costly misunderstandings later on. Include details of time-scales, delivery requirements and what input you will have. Discuss the brief with the supplier to ensure they understand it all.

Manage the relationship carefully

Too many organisations put in all this work to hire the best supplier and then think that's the job done. It is of course only the beginning. Any relationship requires work, and you should put almost as much work into the relationships you have with your suppliers as you do into those with your customers.

Ensure you allocate enough time to the management of the relationship. Hold regular meetings to discuss progress and to plan ahead. Keep them fully updated on your priorities so they can meet your needs. Build slack into your time-scales for the inevitable delays.

Evaluate your relationships regularly. Set aside time to check how well they are working, as well as to keep abreast of the market, so you're always aware of your options. That way you can be certain that you are always getting the maximum value from your suppliers.

Even when you are skilled at managing your outgoings, there will be times in a growing business when more money is necessary. The next chapter will give you insights as to where to get it. First, we conclude this chapter with a look at a company whose fortunes were transformed by suppliers and advisers.

Case study
Capulet

The most radical redesign of the ballet pointe shoe in over 350 years is set to transform the health and fitness of ballerinas. It has also proved to Michael Thoraval, MD of London-based shoe manufacturer Capulet, that external advisers can do more than impose costs – they can transform a business.

Thoraval founded Capulet in 2003. The company employs seven people in a Barnet head office and Covent Garden shop. By 2007 it was turning over £200,000 a year and selling over 12,000 traditional pairs of ballet shoes each year, supplying top dancers at the Royal Ballet and amateur dancers all over the world.

While this was a good start to the business Thoraval wanted to take it further. 'Everyone in the industry has been manufacturing shoes in the same way for more than 300 years,' he says. 'The process uses hessian, paper and paste to create shoes that are notoriously uncomfortable and frequently cause long-lasting damage to dancers. I knew there had to be a better way, but I needed direction and support to help me realise my vision.'

He spent a long time searching for a new material, but had no success, until he saw an article about D3o in a Sunday newspaper. He knew immediately that he had found the right material. However, that was when the real challenge began: to find a way of using it to make a ballet shoe.

He found half a dozen engineers through Google searches and wrote to them outlining his plans. Four responded and he asked them all to quote. The one he wanted to use was too expensive, so he went to the Manufacturing Advisory Service (MAS), a government-backed scheme that advises and assists UK manufacturing companies.

MAS helped finance the innovation work and Capulet has now launched the Capulet D3o, a revolutionary new pointe shoe that actively engages a ballerina's foot as she dances. This dramatically reduces stress and gives her greater freedom of movement. Moreover, the shoe lasts up to six times longer than traditional ballet shoes.

Thoraval explains why this is such an important step forward: 'Lower leg injuries in dancers such as shin splints, ankle sprains and achilles tendonitis result from relying on shoes alone to control and protect the foot. My D3o pointe shoe uses polymers that actively engage the foot during dancing. This ensures a better fit, greater comfort, and, critically for professional ballerinas, a lower risk of injury and enhanced balletic performance.'

This year the company expects to turn over £600,000, and it has a £1.3 million target for the next three years. This project has also made Thoraval much more enthusiastic about working with consultants. He says: 'Without the help of MAS I could not have got it to market in the time I have. We've discovered that we're too small to have the know-how internally, so it makes a lot of sense to bring in external experts.'

He concludes with this advice for how to make a success of these relationships:

'We succeeded because we had a clear vision of what we wanted to achieve. It's vital to work this out early on, and then to convey it to your external advisers, so that they can share your vision. Also, you need to be tenacious. Keep searching for the right suppliers and don't give up.'

Key points

→ It is important to keep costs under control, but remember that
growth requires ongoing investment in people and marketing.

→ Look into cutting your tax bill, but ensure you stay within the law.

→ Know what you spend on fuel and energy, and implement
measures to reduce not only the amount you pay per unit, but
also the number of units that you consume.

→ Get better value from your suppliers by knowing what you want to
buy, picking the right suppliers, agreeing mutually beneficial deals
and managing the relationships effectively.

Next steps

What action will you take to apply the information in this chapter? By
when will you do it?

_____

_____

_____

_____

Whoever said money can't buy happiness simply didn't know where to go shopping. Bo Derek

Financing growth

Chapter Twelve

Don't miss a trick

At some point in your growth you will almost certainly need to get your hands on more money. You may be a very cash-rich business or you may have your own sources of money. In which case, you can count yourself very lucky and probably ignore this chapter.

For most of us, though, at some stage a lack of access to cash becomes a major problem. You might need to pay for new machinery, a large-scale marketing programme or new premises. Whatever it is, once you have begun to grow, you will know that your model works, and this will give you the confidence to invest further.

But will others have the confidence to invest in your business? You would be surprised at the number of entrepreneurs who are running thriving businesses, who are convinced that with an injection of capital they can grow exponentially, but who struggle to raise that capital.

This has become even more of an issue since the credit crunch of late 2007. Even though this has dramatically restricted the flow of finance to business it does not mean that the flow has entirely dried up. There is cash out there – you just need to know how to get your hands on it.

In this chapter I don't cover every aspect of how to manage your finances – you should regularly consult your accountant about that. Instead, I focus on four areas where many entrepreneurs can make a significant improvement to their financial position:

→ Picking the right bank.
→ Using your assets to raise capital.
→ Finding the right investors.
→ Staying on top of cash flow.

Are you with the right bank?

If you need to raise finance, probably the first place you'll go is your bank for an overdraft or a loan. How successful you'll be depends very much on whether or not you've picked the right bank.

Research suggests that few small businesses have found the right bank for them. When the Federation of Private Businesses (FPB) surveyed 3,713 small businesses in early 2007 it found that 75 per cent of those with a turnover below £1 million a year were unhappy with their banks. They were concerned about banks taking personal assets as collateral for business loans, and imposing charges that many see as excessive. They were so disappointed with their banks that more than half of respondents had considered changing bank in the last 12 months.

You might think that it doesn't matter which bank you're with, that they're all as bad as each other. You'd be wrong. There are in fact many differences between what the different banks have to offer, and even the same bank can vary significantly between branches. No matter how long you've been with your bank, at least once a year you should look into your options and ensure you're getting what you need.

Later, Franklin discovered he had made an unwise choice of bank.

There are differences in the rates they charge and offer, in the way they structure their accounts and in their sectoral and geographical specialisations. However, by far the greatest change in the business banking market in the past two or three years has been the rapid growth in direct banking. If you're happy to deal only with your bank online and over the phone you can now save a small fortune in routine bank charges.

You should, though, consider whether or not building a relationship with a bank manager could in the long run help you access finance and provide you with support in more difficult times. To a large extent this decision comes down to how highly you rate your individual bank manager. Is it worth paying charges for their advice and possible future support?

The decision can only be yours, but arm yourself with all the facts. The FPB report makes interesting reading, and provides a ranking of the top business banking providers, as judged by those 3,713 small businesses in early 2007. You can find it at the FPB's website: **www.fpb.org**.

Raising capital – the new way

When you need money for business you probably try your bank for an overdraft or loan, and failing that you might ask friends or family. You might consider remortgaging your property. But what if none of those options are available? What if you've got a great business that you just know will really take off with an injection of capital, but you've exhausted all those finance options?

The answer for a growing number of small businesses is asset-based lending. In a nutshell this is selling the assets your business owns to a third party and then buying them back over time. It's like remortgaging your home, so it's risky, but that isn't deterring a growing band of enthusiasts.

According to the Asset Based Finance Association (ABFA), in the year to March 2008 more than 50,000 UK companies used some form of asset-based finance, more than half of which had a turnover below £1 million. This form of finance used to be viewed as some form of last-chance saloon and an indication that a business was in trouble, but growing numbers of entrepreneurs are using it as an effective way of funding growth.

While banks look for less risky loans to more established companies, so smaller firms are turning to asset-based lenders. However, it is not only the availability of these funds that make them attractive. Many argue that because the financiers spend time investigating a company to understand how the capital will help it grow, they only tend to make sensible deals, and so there is less risk involved.

So, what assets do you have that you can raise finance against?

The most obvious assets are large expensive equipment or machinery. If you own this, then you may be able to release tens of thousands of pounds that are currently tied up in it. The same goes for inventories and property.

Another popular asset is invoices. This involves an invoice financier giving you up to 85 per cent of the value of a sales invoice as soon as you raise it. The invoice financier then chases payment and either keeps it all, including the additional 15 per cent, or takes a service charge from it.

You may even have less tangible assets, such as a strong brand, that you can raise finance against. Whatever assets you use, you must ensure you pick the right finance provider and do the right deal. Be open with your books and, above all else, don't overstretch yourself.

Toolkit

If you want to find out more about asset-based finance, or if you want to contact some financiers, the ABFA should be able to help you: **www.abfa.org.uk** or 020 8332 9955.

Finding the right investors

The final method for raising finance is to sell part of your business. Do you know anyone who could bring not only the injection of cash you need, but also some complementary skills, contacts or experience? Consider your social circle, as well as your professional one. You might find the perfect person among your customers, suppliers or even competitors.

If you don't know anyone who fits the bill you need to start looking. Take another look at the advice in Chapter Eight on finding and exploiting networking opportunities.

Your next best bet probably is a business angel who will invest, usually between £10,000 and £250,000, in return for a share of the business. The share they take will be substantial, but as experienced businesspeople who have probably built and sold their own enterprises they should be able to provide very useful advice and assistance on top of the cash injection.

In the absence of interested individuals you could turn to venture capital funds. These may invest, but will keep a greater distance, expecting only a significant dividend return and a share price increase

Whichever route you take, you will need to get your business and
paperwork in order. Essentially you want to make your business as
attractive as possible. You can do this by changing your business,
doing away with underperforming products or divisions and developing
the most profitable parts, or more simply by ensuring you have accurate and up-to-date records.

These records should include proof of ownership, audited accounts
and profit projections. If you have those to hand you will reassure the
buyer. Think what you would want to see if you were buying into your
business, and then have that to hand ready to show a potential investor.

Seven steps to keeping on top of cash flow

While you're getting excited by all these ways to bring new capital into
your business, it can be all too easy to take your eye off your cash flow.
Indeed, while you're growing your business you can easily overinvest
and suddenly find yourself without enough cash to keep operating.

Poor cash flow is one of the main reasons for business failure, and
following the seven straightforward steps below will help ensure your
plans for growth end in success.

1 Begin by preparing a cash flow forecast

This is simply a projection of all income and expenditure that is
expected for the year. If this shows that you will run out of cash at any
point then you need to take action.

How to Grow Your Business for Entrepreneurs

2 Negotiate good credit terms with your customers and suppliers

The best time to do this is at the beginning of a relationship, but it can be done later on if necessary. Remember that the secret to good negotiation is to give the other person something that has little value to you but that they value. Think laterally about what you can offer. Bear in mind that it may be better for you to be paid less and stay in business.

3 Run credit checks

Avoid the common pitfall of offering credit to a customer with a poor credit history on the promise of future work. They have a poor credit history for a reason: they don't pay their bills on time. So, your promise is likely to remain just that – a promise. You're better off spending your time on customers that will pay on time.

4 Send your invoices out on time

It is remarkable how often busy entrepreneurs forget to invoice for products or services they have delivered. Consider investing in software to help you stay on top of this.

5 Chase debts

Like most people you probably find it a little embarrassing to contact customers and ask for money, especially when the person you have to ask is the person who puts in the original orders and who you deal with regularly. The only way to look at this is that embarrassment is better than insolvency. It can help to establish a set process of emails, phone calls and letters. Above all else, stop delivering to customers who are behind with payments.

6 Minimise excess stock

If you are holding unsold stock you are not only losing out on the potential sale, but you are also paying for warehouse space. Try to plan to reduce this problem as far as possible, and then, if necessary, be prepared to accept a lower price to reduce your exposure to ongoing storage costs.

7 Never relax your focus on cash flow

Although managing cash flow is far from the most exciting part of growing an enterprise, it is one of the most vital. Don't ever get so caught up in long-term development plans that you lose your focus on cash flow.

Key points

→ As well as a good plan, with great ideas and talented people to put it into practice, if you want to grow your business you will, at some point, probably need to raise finance.

→ Getting credit is difficult – especially in the current economic climate – but it is not impossible.

→ Make sure you're with the bank that is right for you.

→ Look into alternative forms of finance.

→ Work hard to make yourself attractive to potential investors.

→ Stay on top of cash flow.

Next steps

What action will you take to apply the information in this chapter? By when will you do it?

_____

_____

_____

_____

How to Grow Your Business for Entrepreneurs

A lawyer with a briefcase can steal more money than a thousand men with guns.

Mario Puzo

Stay on the right side of the law

Chapter Thirteen

Red tape nightmares

The law is an ass, they say. That may well be the case, but it's an ass that will ruin your business if you don't pay sufficient attention to it.

In recent years the UK's entrepreneurs have been subjected to an almost unprecedented barrage of new laws. Many have come from the European Union, and plenty have been sensible laws brought in to protect workers and improve the way we in the UK run our businesses.

This doesn't mean it's been easy for entrepreneurs to keep up. I've spoken to many who have felt like they're being slowly suffocated by red tape. Worryingly, many of them have simply given up trying to comply with all the new rules.

Does this sound familiar? If so, you're playing a dangerous game. It is indeed unlikely that you'll get caught, but if you do the penalties could be devastating. It's easy to ignore the law and to focus all your energies on growing your business, but it's also foolish when you consider that one court case going against you could wipe out all the profits you've made through that growth. It could even be enough to finish your business.

I may be doing you a disservice. You may be highly conscientious and you may stay on top of all the new laws coming through. If so, I apologise. You might still want to take a look at this chapter though. There are so many new laws coming through that you might find one you've not considered yet and that has important repercussions for you.

Ten laws you really should know about

I'm not a lawyer, but I've spoken to ten of the leading business lawyers in the country, and asked them what they see as the most important law for entrepreneurs in your position to be aware of. Here's what each had to say. (If only to prove that I practise what I preach, please note that, while these lawyers are all experts in their field, you should always consult your own lawyer for advice before following any of their advice.)

1 Peter Watson, Managing Partner at Simpson Millar LLP

The law
Employment Equality (Age) Regulations 2006

What it covers
These Regulations formally protect employees from age discrimination. They cover recruitment, terms and conditions, promotions, transfers, dismissals and training.

They introduced a national default retirement age of 65, made compulsory retirement below 65 unlawful and removed upper age limits on unfair dismissal and redundancy. They also gave employees the right to request to work beyond 65.

What you must do to comply
To ensure compliance, even small employers must have an age discrimination policy in place. It must be available to staff. The policy should outline all areas of unlawful discrimination, mention the age limits and be linked in with the firm's disciplinary, grievance and harassment procedures.

Give careful thought not just to employees in the workplace, but also during recruitment. Job adverts and application forms need to be carefully drafted to avoid falling foul of the legislation. Phrases such as 'ambitious young lawyer' or 'mature individual' should no longer be used, and don't ask for an applicant's date of birth. Always keep interview notes to rebut any age-related allegations by unsuccessful applicants.

2 Terry Osborn, Consultant at Nexus Solicitors

The law
Copyright, Designs and Patents Act 1988 (CDPA)

What it covers
CDPA provides that the author of a work is the first owner of any copyright in it, unless the work is made by an employee in the course of their employment, in which case their employer is the first owner of any copyright in the work, subject to any agreement to the contrary.

What you must do to comply

You need to check what you own or think you own. All the rights in a work prepared by a sub- or self-employed contractor will not automatically be owned by the business, even if it has paid for them. This includes work done by web designers, software writers, marketing consultants and many other contractors.

Check any terms and conditions of the contractor and make sure they say what you'd expect. Always put an agreement in place, which need not be complicated, to confirm at least on payment of the contractor's invoice that all rights in the work belong to the business.

Conversely, if your business is the contractor and is commissioned to prepare a work for a client or customer, consider what rights you need to reserve. Often in software development you want to reserve the right to use the software in other applications for other clients, but subject to certain restrictions such as not for a directly competing business. Don't leave these matters to chance as they will almost certainly cause problems at some point if you don't make the position clear.

3 George Wheeler-Carmichael, Partner at Nabarro

The law
The Data Protection Act 1998 (DPA)

What it covers
DPA implements the EC Directive on the protection of individuals' personal data and on the free movement of such data. With the Information Commissioner calling for tougher sanctions on those who misuse personal data and a series of recent headline-grabbing data breach stories, DPA is something that should be at the forefront of all business owners' minds.

What you must do to comply
If your business has control over personal data you must comply with eight principles regarding data processing, data privacy and disclosure. You cannot pass on your legal responsibilities to a third party that processes data on your behalf.

Amongst other requirements, data must be processed fairly and lawfully. This includes getting consent. It must be obtained only for specified and lawful purposes and it must be accurate and kept up to date.

DPA also prohibits transfer of personal data outside the European Economic Area to any place that does not ensure an adequate level of protection for the rights and freedoms of data subjects in relation to the processing of personal data.

There are addition statutory regulations that affect types of direct marketing. For more information and guidance you should refer to the Information Commissioner's website at **www.ico.gov.uk**.

4 Joe Bedford, Partner: Corporate at Stevens & Bolton LLP

The law
Income Tax (Earnings and Pensions) Act 2003 (ITEPA)

What it covers
ITEPA governs the rules regarding Enterprise Management Incentive (EMI) options. These are options on which no income tax or National Insurance contributions will be payable.

You can grant them to your employees if your business qualifies by having assets worth less than £30 million, and by having no more than £3 million shares under option at the date of grant of each option. The tax advantage applies if the exercise price is not less than the market value of shares at grant.

How you can take advantage
You can use EMI options to recruit, retain and motivate employees. They can also be used to help align the interests of senior employees with those of shareholders, by encouraging senior employees to consider the best interests of shareholders in their management of the business.

EMI options can be structured in different ways. For example, the employee's ability to exercise the options can be based on them meeting certain performance targets. Or the employee may only be able to exercise them in the event of a sale.

5 Lucy Handford, Senior Associate: Corporate at Stevens & Bolton LLP

The law

Finance Bill 2008 (to introduce amendments to the Taxation of Chargeable Gains Act 1992)

What it covers

As of 6 April 2008, taper relief, which reduced the amount of capital gain, for example on the sale of shares, chargeable to capital gains tax (CGT), was abolished.

Previously, if someone had sold shares in an unlisted trading company, which they had held for at least two years, taper relief would operate to tax the gain on disposal at an effective rate of 10 per cent. The Finance Bill 2008 introduced a flat rate of 18 per cent of CGT regardless of the type of asset or the period of ownership.

To appease the critics of this abolition of taper relief, the Government introduced a new relief, known as entrepreneurs' relief. This relief provides a lifetime allowance of £1 million of qualifying capital gains. Four-ninths of the qualifying gains will be exempt from CGT. At current rates this gives an effective rate of 10 per cent of CGT.

What you must do to take advantage

Ensure that the shareholding and corporate structure are set up so that, if possible, you can take advantage of entrepreneurs' relief.

The rules governing entrepreneurs' relief are more restrictive than those governing taper relief, so you should obtain legal advice, but broadly, on the disposal of shares, in order to qualify for the entrepreneur's relief the following conditions need to apply:

1 The shares being sold must be shares in a trading company or the holding company of a trading company.

2 For the period of one year prior to disposal, the individual must have:

   (a) been an officer or employee of the company (or another member of the group); and

   (b) held at least 5 per cent of the ordinary share capital which permits them to exercise at least 5 per cent of the voting rights.

6 Lucy Becker, Partner at Lawrence Stephens Solicitors

The law

Privacy and Electronic Communications Regulations, 2002 and 2003

What it covers

The 2002 E-commerce Regulations govern the sale of goods and services to customers by electronic means. They also apply to online advertisements and to businesses that manage electronic content for customers.

Further Regulations came into force in December 2003, with the UK's implementation of the EU Directive on Privacy and Electronic Communications. These were intended to combat the growing problem of 'junk' email communications and the unauthorised collection of personal data.

What you must do to comply

The 2002 Regulations impose two particular requirements on entrepreneurs. Firstly, where a contract is formed by electronic means, customers should be able to print and store a copy of the terms and conditions. Second, electronic advertisements must be clearly recognisable as such when they are sent to customers, and it must be possible to identify the person who sent the communication.

As for the 2003 Regulations, entrepreneurs who send direct marketing communications by email must make their identity clear in that communication. They must also obtain an individual's consent before emailing them any unsolicited advertising.

Existing customers are considered to be legitimate targets as long as the offer relates to products and services similar to those that they have previously purchased. It is essential, however, to provide all recipients with the ability to opt out of receiving further communications.

Finally, the privacy regulations also govern the use of cookies on websites. You are not prohibited from gathering information about website traffic, but you must provide visitors to your website with information about cookies, including instructions on how to disable them.

7 Stuart McBride, Partner and Head of Employment at TLT

The law
Unfair dismissal, section 94 of the Employment Rights Act 2006

What it covers
This is the key employment right in the UK. The maximum compensation for unfair dismissal is currently £63,000 for loss of earnings plus a fixed award of up to £9,900 based on pay, age and service.

Although the average compensation award is a lot lower, claims are still worth avoiding because of the uncertainty and hassle involved. In addition, each side generally pays their own costs in the employment tribunal, so just defending a claim can be expensive.

Employees usually need to have given 51 weeks' service to get unfair dismissal protection. There are a few exceptions to this rule, including dismissals on health and safety or trade union grounds, or where there may be an element of discrimination involved.

What you must do to comply
Use the 51 weeks to discover whether or not someone is right for your business. If you dismiss them after that date, make sure you can show that the reason for dismissal was serious enough to justify dismissal, and also that you followed a fair procedure.

Although by no means impossible, both issues can be tricky in practice, and tribunals are not always consistent in their approach. In addition, the process, especially if dealing with underperformance, can be very slow. Taking advice early is generally a good idea. ACAS (**www.acas.org.uk**) is a good source of free guidance, or alternatively use a lawyer with expertise in the area.

8 Graham Shaw, Partner at TLT

The law
Employment contracts/Provision of employment particulars, section 1 of Employment Rights Act 2006

What it covers

This Act requires all employers to detail in writing to their employees all the key particulars of their employment within two months of an employee starting employment. Failure to comply allows an employee to apply to a tribunal to determine what the terms are, and in some circumstances can lead to compensation for other claims being increased.

What you must do to comply

Provide all employees with this information in writing within two months of them starting. You must cover pay, hours, job title or duties, holidays, sickness, notice period and a reference to the applicable disciplinary and grievance procedures. This statement of terms is usually best provided in a contract of employment.

Remember that the real reason for issuing a statement of terms is to protect your business. The law still gives employers quite a lot of leeway as to how contracts are drafted, so you can use them to give the business flexibility in terms of duties, hours and place of work. You can also make sure potentially contentious areas such as sick pay, overtime and commission are clear cut.

You can even include more technical provisions, which protect intellectual property, confidential information and, for a limited period, your customer base. If you want to include these you will need to obtain legal advice.

9 Roger Pointon, Partner: Corporate at Hill Dickinson

The law

Companies (Registrar, Languages and Trading Disclosures) Regulations 2006

What it covers

These Regulations are part of the programme to reform company law under the Companies Act 2006. They oblige all companies and limited liability partnerships to provide specific information on their websites and electronic communications. The Regulations came into force on 3 January 2007.

The Regulations aim to encourage consumer confidence in using the internet for retail and commercial purposes. Prior to the Regulations, there was widespread agreement that websites provided unsatisfactory levels of detail about the site owner, individual or company.

What you must do to comply

Clearly state the following information on all electronic business communication, such as faxes, emails and text messages:

→ Full corporate name (as it appears in the Memorandum of Association).

→ Place of registration.

→ Registered number.

→ Registered office address.

→ In the case of an investment company, the fact that it is an investment company.

→ In the case of a limited company exempt from the obligation to use the word 'limited' as part of its name, the fact that it is a limited company.

You don't need to include the information listed above on every page of your website. It's best included in the 'Legal Information' or 'About Us' section.

10 Christopher Parr at Collyer Bristow LLP

The law

The Unfair Contract Terms Act 1977

What it covers

This law deals with both business-to-business and business-to-consumer agreements and has two major points of particular relevance to small businesses, both as sellers and buyers of goods and services.

The first is a provision which prohibits, absolutely, the exclusion of liability for death or injury which is caused by your negligence or the business's negligence. So, for example, if you or your employees work on a site and injure the client or anyone else, if negligence is proved against you or your employee, then you cannot rely on any contract term to avoid liability for damages.

The second is the strict requirement, at least in B2C contracts, that the supplier cannot have the right to supply goods which: either do not correspond to the description, or any sample, given at, or prior to, the point of sale; or are not fit for their purpose. In B2B agreements, this restriction is relaxed to allow reasonable limits and exclusions. In this context, if the parties are of unequal bargaining power, and/or if the seller insists on applying its standard terms of business, then 'reasonableness' will be difficult to prove.

What you must do to comply

To protect yourself against any liability you should not rely on a clause in your contracts. You should carry insurance which will cover you and your employees against any claims.

Key points

→ Ignore the law at your peril.

→ Establish an age discrimination policy.

→ Find out exactly what copyrights you own and patents you hold.

→ Comply with all data protection legislation.

→ Look into how Enterprise Management Incentive options could benefit you.

→ Take advantage of entrepreneurs' relief on capital gains tax.

→ On electronic communications provide all necessary information and respect recipients' privacy.

→ Know what constitutes unfair dismissal and follow procedures to avoid it.

→ Give all staff detailed statements of terms.

→ Carry insurance to protect against all liabilities.

Next steps

What action will you take to apply the information in this chapter? By when will you do it?

_____

_____

_____

_____

The end – and the beginning

So, how did it end for Tom Gorman, the MD of TDG Print, who we saw back in the Introduction wondering how he was ever going to grow his business? Well, it did end well for him. First of all, he recognised his own abilities and limitations.

'Back in 1998 I thought business was all about sales,' he says. 'I've learnt that there's much more to it than that and so, while my strength is sales, I've realised that to grow my business I need to surround myself with people who are good at getting things done. I need people who are strong in areas like human resources, finance and process engineering.'

He deliberately hired people with those skills. Recruiting them wasn't easy. In fact Gorman describes it as his greatest challenge. 'It's easy to hire people who are just like you, so you end up with a room full of entrepreneurs and nothing gets done. You need workers, too. A crucial lesson for me was not being afraid of hiring people who are smarter than I am.'

To overcome this difficulty he split his business into clear divisions, so he could recruit people for specific jobs. However, even with good people in place, Gorman has, like many entrepreneurs, found it difficult to delegate to them. He admits that there have been plenty of times where he's heard one of his staff on the phone to a client or a prospect and has wanted to jump in.

'I've had to learn to hold back and realise that they're just doing it in a different way,' he says. 'Now I ask questions first before jumping in and criticising.'

He also works hard to involve his 30 employees in his plans for the business and its future. 'We have monthly meetings where I explain what's going on in the business and demonstrate to everyone how what they do affects the organisation as a whole. It really helps to get them to buy into our future.'

Doing all this has had an impressive effect. In fact it has transformed the business. Gorman says: 'Having talented and committed staff means that things get done when I'm not here, and it frees me up to get out and sell the business.'

The firm now works for big-name clients like The Body Shop and Hasbro, and Gorman reports that a significant change has been in how those clients see his company: 'We're much more of a trusted partner these days, as opposed to a supplier that is kept at arm's length. It's because we've got the people and the processes to deliver exactly what those clients need.'

All this has led to phenomenal growth. A decade ago, TDG Print was turning over a few hundred thousand a year, and Gorman wasn't sure it would ever do much more than that. Now it turns over £9 million a year.

You can do this, too

At the start of this book I said that there are thousands of businesses that struggle to grow beyond their initial start-up phase. They reach a plateau, beyond which they cannot grow. There are, though, many companies that do succeed in growing beyond this point. TDG Print is one of them, and throughout this book we've seen many other examples.

I hope that my book has given you practical ideas for how you, too, can grow your business. It's not impossible. Difficult certainly, but not impossible.

Perhaps you've read this far and seen the logic of what I'm saying, but still don't feel it applies to your business. Perhaps you've been struggling to grow your business for so long that on some level you believe it's impossible, that there's something about your business which means it just can't grow any further.

If so, please take a few minutes to consider this story.

For a long time it was widely believed that it was impossible for humans to run a mile in less than four minutes. In 1945 Sweden's Gunder Haegg had achieved 4 minutes and 1.4 seconds. For eleven years afterwards athletes tried to break that time, but without success. Doctors, runners and experts worldwide concluded that it was beyond the capacity of the human body – it just couldn't be done.

How to Grow Your Business for Entrepreneurs

Then on 6 May 1954 Roger Bannister ran a mile in 3 minutes and 59.4 seconds. He proved that it could be done.

John Landy, another runner, had achieved a personal best of 4 minutes and 2 seconds and had previously described the four-minute barrier as 'like a wall'. Only 56 days after Bannister broke through that wall, Landy followed him. By the end of 1957 sixteen other runners had also broken the four-minute mile.

Bannister had proved that there was no physical barrier to humans breaking the four-minute mile. There had only ever been a psychological one. As soon as all those athletes believed they could do it, they achieved something which up until then they had thought was impossible.

You might have been trying for years to grow your business, without success. But that doesn't mean it's impossible. Try again. Take just one idea from this book and implement it over the next month. If it works, or even if it doesn't, dip in again, find another good idea and try it out. Do this again and again, over a year, and it will work – you will grow your business.

What will you do next?

It takes a lot of hard work to grow a business. I hope this book will make it a little easier for you, but still you'll have to put in a lot of hard work.

Once you've done it you'll discover a whole world of opportunities opening up before you. You'll own a business that will run itself without the need for your constant involvement. You will also be one of the very few people who know exactly what it takes to grow a business.

You will at that point have more freedom than you ever thought possible, and you'll face one of the most difficult decisions in your life: what will you do next?

Gorman bought a deli and is enjoying running that alongside his first business. Some of the other entrepreneurs I've profiled in this book have chosen to keep growing their first businesses. It can become an addictive process. Others are preparing to sell up and start sipping cocktails in the sunshine.

Whatever you choose to do at that point, you'll have earned it, and I wish you good luck getting there. Finally, remember to have fun while you're doing it.

Index